Creative Metaphor, Evaluation, and Emotion in Conversations about Work

This book explores the roles played by creative and conventional metaphor in expressing positive and negative evaluation within a particular workplace, drawing on interviews with 31 current and former employees of the British Civil Service.

Metaphor is often used to express evaluation but relatively few studies have investigated the ways in which metaphor is used to evaluate personal emotionally charged experiences. The volume explores how metaphor serves a predominantly evaluative function, with creatively used metaphors often more likely than conventional metaphors to perform an evaluative function, particularly when the evaluation is negative or ambiguous. The findings provide a deeper understanding of the relationship between evaluation, creativity, and metaphor. Examples, including military metaphors and family metaphors, show how creativity often comes through subverting the norms of use of a particular metaphor category, or altering the valence from its conventional use. The study elucidates the myriad ways in which people push at the boundaries of linguistic creativity in their efforts to describe the qualitative nature of their experiences.

Demonstrating how metaphor can be a powerful tool for the nuanced expression of complex and ambiguous evaluation, this book will appeal to researchers interested in better understanding metaphor, creativity, evaluation, and workplace cultures.

Jeannette Littlemore is a Professor of Applied Linguistics in the Department of English Language and Linguistics at the University of Birmingham, UK. Her research focuses on the role played by creative and conventional metaphor and metonymy in the sharing of emotional experiences.

Sarah Turner is an Assistant Professor of Cognitive Linguistics in the Research Centre for Arts, Memory and Communities at Coventry University, UK. Her research focuses on the analysis of figurative language production to provide insights into physical, psychological, and social experiences.

Penelope Tuck is a Professor of Accounting, Public Finance, and Policy at Birmingham Business School, University of Birmingham, UK. Her research area is accounting from a social and institutional perspective. She focuses on engaged research and covers sites such as taxation, central government, and the health sector.

Routledge Focus on Applied Linguistics

Moving Beyond the Grammatical Syllabus
Practical Strategies for Content-Based Curriculum Design
Jason Martel

Contesting Grand Narratives of the Intercultural
Adrian Holliday

Sustainability of Blended Language Learning Programs
Technology Integration in English for Academic Purposes
Cynthia Nicholas Palikat and Paul Gruba

Discourses of Borders and the Nation
A Discourse-Historical Analysis
Massimiliano Demata

Health Disparities and the Applied Linguist
Maricel G. Santos, Rachel Showstack, Glenn Martínez, Drew Colcher, Dalia Magaña

Instruction Giving in Online Language Lessons
A Multimodal (Inter)action Analysis
Müge Satar and Ciara R. Wigham

Language Policy and the Future of Europe
A Conversation with Seán Ó Riain
Alice Leal and Seán Ó Riain

Creative Metaphor, Emotion and Evaluation in Conversations about Work
Jeannette Littlemore, Sarah Turner and Penelope Tuck

For more information about this series, please visit: https://www.routledge.com/Routledge-Focus-on-Applied-Linguistics/book-series/RFAL

Creative Metaphor, Evaluation, and Emotion in Conversations about Work

Jeannette Littlemore, Sarah Turner, and Penelope Tuck

LONDON AND NEW YORK

First published 2024
by Routledge
4 Park Square, Milton Park, Abingdon, Oxon, OX14 4RN

and by Routledge
605 Third Avenue, New York, NY 10158

Routledge is an imprint of the Taylor & Francis Group, an informa business

© 2024 Jeannette Littlemore, Sarah Turner, and Penelope Tuck

The right of Jeannette Littlemore, Sarah Turner, and Penelope Tuck to be identified as authors of this work has been asserted in accordance with sections 77 and 78 of the Copyright, Designs and Patents Act 1988.

All rights reserved. No part of this book may be reprinted or reproduced or utilised in any form or by any electronic, mechanical, or other means, now known or hereafter invented, including photocopying and recording, or in any information storage or retrieval system, without permission in writing from the publishers.

Trademark notice: Product or corporate names may be trademarks or registered trademarks, and are used only for identification and explanation without intent to infringe.

Library of Congress Cataloging-in-Publication Data
Names: Littlemore, Jeannette, author. | Turner, Sarah (Professor of cognitive linguistics) author. | Tuck, Penelope, author.
Title: Creative metaphor, emotion and evaluation in conversations about work / authored by Jeannette Littlemore, Sarah Turner, Penelope Tuck.
Description: New York, NY: Routledge, 2024. | Series: Routledge focus on applied linguistics | Includes bibliographical references and index.
Identifiers: LCCN 2023025301 | ISBN 9781032199788 (hardback) | ISBN 9781032199788 (paperback) | ISBN 9781003262862 (ebook)
Subjects: LCSH: Metaphor–Social aspects. | Language and emotions–Great Britain. | Language in the workplace–Great Britain. | Creative thinking–Great Britain. | Employees–Great Britain–Language. | Civil service–Great Britain.
Classification: LCC P301.5.M48 L57 2024 | DDC 401/.43–dc23/eng/20230725
LC record available at https://lccn.loc.gov/2023025301

ISBN: 978-1-032-19978-8 (hbk)
ISBN: 978-1-032-20247-1 (pbk)
ISBN: 978-1-003-26286-2 (ebk)

DOI: 10.4324/9781003262862

Typeset in Times New Roman
by Deanta Global Publishing Services, Chennai, India

Contents

Acknowledgements   *vii*

1 'I'm sort of running on this soapy conveyor belt with people throwing wet sponges at me and I've got this sodding great elastic band attached to my back': Why look at creative metaphor, evaluation and emotion in conversations about work?   1

The role played by metaphor in the sharing of emotional experiences 2
Are creative or conventional metaphors more likely to be used for evaluation? 2
Is (creative) metaphor more likely to be used for positive or negative evaluation? 5
Previous studies of the role played by metaphor in the workplace, and the approach taken in this study 6
A final (but important) comment on the nature of 'creative metaphor' 8
The context of the study 9
Research questions 10
References 10

2 'I'm surprised anybody can hear anything going on for the crashing of all of these elephants in the room': Methodology and taxonomy of creative metaphor types   14

Introduction 14
Participants and interview procedure 14
Procedure used for the identification of metaphor 14

    Procedure used for the identification of creative uses of metaphor and taxonomy of creative uses of metaphor 17
    Procedure used for the identification of positive and negative evaluation 32
    Conclusion 33
    References 33

3 'She did the traditional sort of chuck it all up in the air, so get all the deckchairs and throw them up in the air, cause chaos for a year and a half and then leave': To what extent are creative metaphors used to perform evaluation and how do creative and conventional metaphors relate to one another?   35

    Introduction 35
    To what extent is metaphor used to express evaluation in conversations about work? Is the use of metaphor more likely to be associated with positive or negative evaluation? And do creative and conventional metaphor differ in terms of the extent to which they express (positive or negative) evaluation? 36
    Which metaphors were used to perform what kinds of evaluation, and how were they employed? 37
    Conclusion 58
    Note 58
    References 59

4 Concluding: 'As people rotate round, some will spin off the merry-go-round and shoot off back to the private sector'   60

    References 61

    Index   *63*

Acknowledgements

We would like to express our gratitude to our participants, who gave up their time to speak to us about their experiences in the Civil Service. Big thanks also go to Abigail Kinsella for helping us to develop and implement the framework for analysing different kinds of creative metaphor.

1 'I'm sort of running on this soapy conveyor belt with people throwing wet sponges at me and I've got this sodding great elastic band attached to my back'

Why look at creative metaphor, evaluation and emotion in conversations about work?

> *My role here [is]a bit like an It's a Knockout game. I'm sort of running on this soapy conveyor belt with people throwing wet sponges at me and I've got this sodding great elastic band attached to my back.*

The above quote is an extract from an interview with a senior British Civil Servant. He has just been asked how he feels about his role, and how he prioritises different tasks within it. He is presumably aiming to convey his frustration with the competing demands on his time. In order to do this, he uses a metaphor in which he compares his job with the television programme 'It's a Knockout'. This programme, which was aired in the 1970s and 1980s in the UK, featured teams from towns or cities across the UK, who competed in a series of absurd, undignified, and humiliating challenges, often dressed in large foam rubber suits. During these challenges (which were often impossible to complete), contestants would sometimes have soft projectiles thrown at them. Both the speaker and the interviewer were of the generation to remember this programme. By alluding to this programme, the speaker manages to convey a number of evaluations of his current position, namely that although the goal may ultimately be worthwhile, the day-to-day challenge is virtually impossible, all sorts of impediments are thrown in his way, he feels frustrated, and feels as if he is deliberately being set up to fail and to look ridiculous.

This speaker is using creative metaphor to convey his strong negative evaluation of a highly emotionally charged workplace experience. His choice to do so is likely to have been motivated by the fact this allowed him to create a highly imageable, visceral, and memorable image which allowed him to fully convey his felt experience. But how widespread is this practice? Is there something about metaphor that makes it particularly apt for the expression of evaluation? Is the use of metaphor particularly likely to be associated with

DOI: 10.4324/9781003262862-1

emotionally charged negative evaluation? And do more negative experiences drive the production of creative metaphor? These questions are of central interest to us and form the focus of this book.

The role played by metaphor in the sharing of emotional experiences

The fact that metaphor has a strong physical and visceral basis renders it particularly conducive to the sharing of emotional experiences (Gibbs, 2022). This is because metaphor *concretely demonstrates* what that experience was like, and listeners are able to infer the communicative meanings by imagining themselves performing the actions alluded to by the specific words employed by the speakers (Colston & Gibbs, 2021). Metaphors allow the listener to simulate the physical experience through which the abstract concept or feeling is being expressed. This feature of metaphor also allows the speaker to convey how they felt about the experience, what emotions they experienced, and ultimately how they evaluated that experience.

Emotion and evaluation are closely linked (Martin & White, 2005) and the fact that metaphor plays a key role in expressing emotions is related to the fact that it often serves an evaluative function. Indeed, the important role played by metaphor in performing evaluation has been discussed at length in both the metaphor literature and in the evaluation literature. Within the metaphor literature, two leading researchers, Cameron (2003) and Semino (2008, 31) list evaluation as being one of the key functions performed by metaphor in discourse. Findings from corpus-based studies also point to a strong relationship between metaphor and evaluation. In his corpus-based study of sensory language, Winter (2019) found that the more emotionally valenced an adjective was, the more likely it was used in a synesthetic metaphor. Through an extensive corpus-based study of fixed expressions and idioms in English, Moon (1998) found that metaphorical idioms are significantly more likely to serve an evaluative function than non-metaphorical idioms. Finally, in her corpus-based study of French and Japanese learners of English, Turner (2014) found that when learners used metaphor in their written work, this was frequently to perform evaluative functions. Within the evaluation literature, both Simon-Vandenbergen (2003) and Bednarek (2009) provide numerous examples of metaphorical expressions that serve explicitly evaluative functions, whilst other researchers see metaphor as a valuable resource for expressing evaluation in a more covert, implicit way (Hood & Martin, 2005; Liu, 2018; Martin & White, 2005).

Are creative or conventional metaphors more likely to be used for evaluation?

One cannot help but notice that the metaphor in the opening quote is highly creative. Office work is not normally compared to participation in humiliating game shows. By drawing on this creative comparison, the speaker is able to extend the metaphorical scene to incorporate other features such as wet sponges and the idea that there is an elastic band holding him back. These features contribute to the intensity of the overall felt experience of the metaphorical scene being described.

However, not all metaphor is used in such a creative way as this; most metaphor is highly conventional and reflects established ways of seeing things. This is because it is virtually impossible to talk and think about abstract concepts without recourse to metaphor and sets of conventionalised metaphorical correspondences (Johnson, 2013; Lakoff & Johnson, 1980). For example, in English we talk about moving forward through time as if we were moving forward through space so we might 'look ahead to tomorrow' or 'think back to what we were doing yesterday'. Similarly, we talk about emotional closeness in terms of 'warmth', possibly because we experience a co-occurrence of warmth and affection as infants.

Although many conventionalised metaphorical relationships, such as those we have just mentioned, are universal, others have been shown to vary across cultures and communities. Groups of people who work together towards a common interest are often referred to as discourse communities, and discourse communities have been shown to develop their own ways of talking or 'discourse' which are often characterised by the metaphors they use. This has led some to argue that the use of metaphor is a key defining characteristic of discourse communities (Partington, 1998). Within a discourse community, people are socialised into using particular metaphors which make a powerful contribution to 'in-group' language (Deignan et al., 2013).

In addition to this, much research on metaphor has emphasised the need to see metaphor not as a static phenomenon but as playing a dynamic role in the way in which people seek to make sense of the world (Gibbs, 2019). This view of metaphor is also prevalent in work that seeks to understand the ways in which metaphorical thinking shapes behaviour within organisations:

> The danger with an excessive concern for classification is that it can keep us in an abstract intellectual space, placing too much emphasis on the epistemological aspects of metaphor as opposed to understanding and dealing with its role in the interactive, emergent process of engagement through which people are seeking to deal with their world. This process of emergence is always two-way and involves an interaction between the ontological elements of a situation (i.e. the specific events, people and other circumstances with which one is interacting), and the metaphorical mode of engagement through which one is attempting to understand, shape and act in relation to that situation.
>
> (Morgan, 2016, 1037)

Thus, in addition to serving as a device that people use to build a community mindset, metaphor can also be used to disrupt prevalent thinking, challenge the status quo, and critique dominant cultures and practices (Heracleous & Jacobs, 2011). One might conclude from this that when people are critiquing aspects of their workplace cultures, they may use metaphor to 'break free' of the dominant culture and to express different ways of thinking about it. This view of metaphor suggests that it may play an important role when people are evaluating their experiences of their workplace environments.

There is evidence to suggest that creative metaphor is particularly useful in performing evaluation, in comparison to conventional metaphor. In previous work, where we explored the role played by metaphor in expressing evaluation in film reviews, we (Fuoli et al., 2021) found that approximately half of the metaphors in the review corpus performed an evaluative function, with creative metaphors being significantly more likely to perform an evaluative function than conventional metaphors. One reason for this might be that evaluation is an emotionally charged activity (Musch & Klauer, 2003). In their model of appraisal, Martin and White (2005) postulate three types of evaluation: 'affect' (which refers to one's personal emotional state), 'judgement' (the social or ethical appraisal of other people's behaviour), and 'appreciation' (evaluation of the aesthetics of stimuli). The first of these forms of appraisal is clearly emotional, but we would also argue that emotional responses play an important role in the two other forms of appraisal which refer to subjective responses to other people's behaviour or to stimuli. Metaphorical language is often used to express emotions and metaphor has, in turn been shown to influence people's emotions (Hendricks et al., 2018; Thibodeau et al., 2017). Emotion has been shown to be a key driver in the production of creative metaphor in particular (Russ, 2013). People have been found to use more metaphor, particularly creative metaphor, when writing about emotional experiences than when talking about non-emotional experiences (Williams-Whitney et al., 1992), and it is the first-hand experience of these emotions which provides the motivation for creative metaphor production (MacCormac, 1986). One can hardly fail to notice the highly charged emotional content of the quote at the beginning of this chapter, as well as the fact that the evaluation is clearly negative, and the fact that the speaker is drawing on an imagined physical experience to describe his emotions.

Crucially, Fainsilber, and Ortony (1987) found that people produced more metaphor, and particularly creative metaphor, when describing intense emotional experiences. They propose three hypotheses to explain this finding: the compactness hypothesis, the vividness hypothesis, and the inexpressibility hypothesis. The compactness hypothesis refers to the idea that metaphor provides a way of conveying a large amount of information in a more concise way than literal speech does. The vividness hypothesis holds that metaphors can provide richer and more detailed accounts of experience than literal language, while the inexpressibility hypothesis holds that 'metaphors provide a way of expressing ideas that would be extremely difficult to convey using literal language' (Gibbs, 1994, 124). All of these come to the fore in the expression of intense, personal experiences. Such experiences are often difficult to express *without* recourse to metaphor in general, and creative metaphor in particular.

Is (creative) metaphor more likely to be used for positive or negative evaluation?

Another feature of the opening quote that we have not yet commented on in detail is the fact that the evaluation is largely negative. The speaker is using a somewhat unpleasant and humiliating scene in order to represent his experiences at work. Might it therefore be the case that metaphor is more likely to be used for negative evaluation than for positive evaluation? In her study of the role played by metaphor in educational settings, Cameron (2003) found that it was more likely to be used to perform negative evaluation than positive evaluation. Similarly, in our aforementioned study of film reviews, we found that metaphorical evaluation was significantly more negative than non-metaphorical evaluation (Fuoli et al., 2021).

But what about the relationship between the polarity of the evaluation and the creativity of the metaphors that are used to express it? Here, we draw again on the relationship between emotion and evaluation. In Fainsilber and Ortony's aforementioned study, people were found to be more likely to use creative metaphor when describing intense emotions as opposed to actions and less intense emotions, and this difference was significantly more marked for positive emotions than for negative emotions. In a related study, Ortony and Fainsilber (1987) asked participants to describe their experiences of positive and negative emotions and then to describe what they did in response to those emotions. They found that respondents used more creative metaphor when describing intense emotions than when describing the actions associated with them, and that when metaphor was used in the descriptions of actions, more metaphors were produced for actions relating to negative than to positive emotions. In our aforementioned study of film reviews (Fuoli et al., 2021), we found that creative metaphor was more likely than conventional metaphor to be associated with evaluation, and in his study of sensory metaphors, Winter (2019) found that sensory references that involved synaesthetic metaphor were more likely to perform evaluation than sensory references that did not. However, neither of these studies found polarity to be a factor.

A key difference between the aforementioned studies (especially Fuoli et al. 2021) and the study reported in this book is that the focus of the aforementioned studies was on the use of creative and conventional metaphors to evaluate subject matter that is relatively distant to the speaker or writer. In the study described in this book, we focus on the ways in which people use creative and conventional metaphor to evaluate experiences that are very personal to them, and which as such may have been emotionally charged. For this reason, we may therefore encounter different findings. There is some evidence from work outside the field of metaphor to suggest that the polarity of an emotional experience can affect the creativity of the language that is used to express it, although findings and theories in the area are mixed. For example, Nijstad, De Dreu, Rietzschel, and Baas (2010) suggest that activating positive mood states in participants enhances creativity because they stimulate flexibility, while activating negative mood states can enhance creativity because they stimulate persistence. Interestingly, negative emotional experiences in the workplace have been found to trigger the production of creative outputs, especially if they are immediately followed by more positive emotional experiences (Bledow et al., 2013). One reason for this may be the fact that negative experiences are more varied, yield more complex representations, and engage a wider response repertoire (Rozin & Royzman, 2001). This suggests that people may draw on more creative resources when endeavouring to express or share these experiences.

From this brief literature review, we might postulate that metaphor plays an important role in performing evaluation, that creative metaphor plays a particularly important role in this respect, and that negative evaluations of personal emotionally charged experiences are likely to be performed by metaphor in general, and by creative metaphor in particular. These are the key issues that we explore in this book. Traditional analyses of metaphor in everyday language use have not tended to distinguish between conventional and creative metaphor. The fact that metaphor can be used in these contrasting ways suggests that when analysts use metaphor as a tool to identify workplace cultures and people's attitudes towards those cultures they should distinguish between the two types of metaphor. By examining the conventional metaphors that people use when talking about their workplace cultures, we can gain insights into workplace cultures. In contrast, by examining the creative metaphors they use we can see how they critique, reflect on, and sometimes challenge the cultures and the status quo. Through using language in novel, interesting ways, speakers draw attention to aspects of their experience which they consider to be particularly salient. The findings from some of the above studies suggest that the valence of the evaluation/emotion may affect the extent to which metaphor is employed and the level of creativity of the metaphor. This is also an interesting area to explore when investigating the use of metaphor to evaluate workplace experiences.

Previous studies of the role played by metaphor in the workplace, and the approach taken in this study

The focus of our study is on the role played by metaphor in conversations about the Civil Service workplace. Metaphors have long been of interest to management and organisational researchers seeking to understand a range of workplace phenomena. They have been employed as a tool for analysing organisational culture (Morgan, 1998; Tsoukas, 1993) and organisational conflict (Tyler & Wilkinson, 2007), workplace culture identity (Vaara et al.,

2003), trade union learning across countries (Cassell & Lee, 2012) and customer abuse in the workplace (Cassell & Bishop, 2019), workplace bullying (Tracy et al., 2006), and the identities of expat workers (Richardson & McKenna, 2000).

Given the wide range of topics to which metaphor analyses have been applied, it is not surprising that researchers have taken different methodological approaches to their study of metaphor. We can identify three main approaches, which here we label metaphor application, metaphor elicitation, and studies of naturally occurring metaphor. We characterise the metaphor application approach as one where the researcher or analyst applies a particular, usually familiar metaphor to a phenomenon to enable a novel or in-depth understanding of that phenomenon. There are numerous examples of this within the management and organisation literature. Recent examples include Hitchner, Schelhas, and Brosius' (2016) use of the metaphors of snake oil, silver buckshot, and terrorists to explore how people talk about wood-based energy in the rural southeastern USA. The second approach is that of metaphor elicitation where the researcher seeks to explicitly create metaphorical data by eliciting metaphors from respondents, for example as part of an interview schedule. One approach is to include a question within an interview schedule that asks an interviewee to think about a metaphor that captures the issue of interest. Examples of this approach include Burrell, Buzzanell, and McMillan's (1992) study of women's experiences of conflict at work, Tracy et al.'s (2006) study of workplace bullying, Tosey, Lawley, and Meese's (2014) clean language exploration of work-life balance, and Cassell and Bishop's (2019) exploration of taxi drivers' experiences of customer abuse. In studies of naturally occurring metaphor, the analyst takes a particular data and examines that data to identify metaphors in use. This approach can be used with a variety of sets of textual or visual data. In the field of business, Gibson and Zellmer-Bruhn's (2001) analysis of teamwork metaphors derived from interview data is an example of this.

The approach taken in this study is akin to this last approach as it is a study of naturally occurring metaphor. We conduct a detailed analysis of the ways in which metaphor is used by UK Civil Servants when talking about their workplace experiences, with a focus on the differences between creative and conventional metaphor use. Within this setting, our first aim is to investigate whether creative metaphors are indeed more likely to perform an evaluative function than conventional metaphors, and if so, whether the evaluation they offer is more likely to be negative. Our second aim is to identify the different types of metaphor that are used to describe workplace experiences and to measure the extent to which each of these types is used to express positive or negative evaluation. Our intention is to build up an overall picture of how metaphor is used to convey evaluation in conversations about work. Our third aim is to compare and contrast creative versus conventional metaphors and assess whether they convey more positive or more negative evaluation, and to explore the different ways in which metaphors are used creatively.

A final (but important) comment on the nature of 'creative metaphor'

In order to conduct this study, it is also necessary to explore what is meant by 'creative metaphor'. At this point, it is useful to consider what 'creativity' means. For an idea to be considered 'creative', it must combine 'novelty' with 'appropriateness' (Carter, 2015). In other words, it needs to have an element of originality but also serve a communicative purpose in an effective manner (Runco & Jaeger, 2012). Traditionally, the distinction between creative and conventional metaphor has been seen as being relatively unproblematic. Usually, a metaphor is considered to be conventional if it has an established meaning that is widely shared by native speakers of the language (see Werkmann Horvat et al., 2022). So, for example, the use of the metaphorical expression 'Claire was in a tight corner' to mean that she was in a difficult situation would be considered conventional in English as most native speakers of English would be familiar with this expression, and definitions along the lines of the one that we have just given can be found in many English dictionaries. In contrast, a creative metaphor involves the identification of a meaningful similarity between two previously unrelated concepts. For example, if instead of saying that Claire was in a tight corner, one were to say that she had found herself 'in a particularly messy plate of tagliatelle', this would constitute an apparent 'novel' or 'creative' metaphor, as difficult situations are not normally compared to plates of tagliatelle.

More recent work in this area has taken the category of 'creative metaphor' and broken it down further, identifying two different kinds of creative metaphor, one of which involves creating a completely new mapping, whilst the other involves incorporating more detail into an existing mapping (Barnden, 2015; Burgers & Ahrens, 2020; Littlemore et al., 2018; Pérez-Sobrino et al., 2021; Werkmann Horvat et al., 2021). For example, Pérez-Sobrino et al. (2021) draw a distinction between 'creative exploitations of one-off source domains' and 'unusual realizations of wide-scope source domains'. As an example of the former, they cite the example of a Norwegian journalist writing that if one is going to be a hero during the Covid pandemic, one should actually 'act like a hedgehog, don't roar like a lion or fight like a giant but roll up in a ball and wait and hope for better times'. They point out that hedgehogs are not conventionally used as a source domain for human behaviour, and that references to hedgehog-like behaviour are likely to be unexpected in the context of the pandemic, which was characterised by references to heroic, war-like behaviour. As an example of incorporating more detail into an existing mapping, they cite an Italian commentator who talked about the need to 'reclaim the soil after the coronavirus fire'. This, they argue, involves a textual and conceptual extension of a conventional source domain, fire, which is often used amongst other things to talk about fast developing problems, such as inflation.

Although this distinction is intuitively plausible, it is not without its problems. The idea of a one-off source domain is particularly problematic because, if we go further up the hierarchy in terms of abstraction, we eventually reach a conventional mapping. To take the hedgehog example, as Pérez-Sobrino et al., themselves point out, metaphorical comparisons between people and animals are not uncommon. Furthermore, the Chambers dictionary gives 'someone whose manners keep others at a distance' and 'an offensive person' as meanings of 'hedgehog' (which, interestingly, is not marked as figurative). So, it appears that hedgehogs are sometimes conventionally used as a source domain for human behaviour, at least in English. Thus, the use of the hedgehog domain does not appear to be a 'one-off' use of this domain, but rather it is more the case that the use of this domain differs from conventional uses. The creativity in this example lies more in the fact that the characteristics associated with this animal are diametrically opposed to the predominant war-like public discourse. The same argument could likely be made for all instances of 'completely' novel metaphors or one-off source domains. For a metaphor to be comprehensible, it must, at some point, draw on some shared knowledge, even if this knowledge is highly schematic or abstract. Later in this book, we propose a taxonomy of creative uses of metaphor that moves beyond this binary distinction. The taxonomy extends that which we proposed for the film reviews data proposed by Fuoli et al. (2021).

The context of the study

The workplace that forms the focus of this study is the UK Civil Service, which is the executive of the UK Government. The UK Civil Service is an unelected body, which serves the Government of the day and is subject to high-profile ministerial criticism (Urban & Thomas, 2022). We explore the language used by 31 current and former senior (deputy directors, directors, and director general level) Civil Servants in interviews about their workplace experiences. The UK Civil Service provides an interesting context for exploring the ways in which people use language when describing the workplace culture and their attitudes towards that culture. Although the UK Civil Service is a place where many people aspire to work, the day-to-day experience of working there presents a number of challenges. There is a strong hierarchical executive leadership (Rhodes, 2007); a wide variety of stakeholders are involved in the business of government so Civil Servants need to be able to deal with uncertainty and vaguely defined performance goals (Chun & Rainey, 2006); and Civil Servants often lack autonomy and control over their work (Bozeman & Feeney, 2014). Given these challenges, one would expect a good deal of evaluative language to be employed when Civil Servants are asked to reflect on their workplace experiences.

Research questions

In this study we explore the roles played by creative and conventional metaphor in evaluating workplace experiences. We aim to answer the following research questions:

1. To what extent is metaphor used to express evaluation in conversations about work?
2. Is the use of metaphor more likely to be associated with positive or negative evaluation?
3. Do creative and conventional metaphor differ in terms of the extent to which they express (positive or negative) evaluation?
4. What forms does creative metaphor take and how is it best distinguished from conventional metaphor?

In order to answer the fourth research question, we investigated the various forms that creative metaphor took in our corpus, which led to the development of a taxonomy of creative metaphor types. This taxonomy, as we will see in Chapter 2, challenges some of the conventional wisdom concerning what is meant by 'creative metaphor'. We use the findings from our study to shed light on what the analysis of metaphor can tell us about implicit cultures and experiences within the UK Civil Service workplace, and how these were evaluated.

References

Barnden, J. A. (2015). Open-ended elaborations in creative metaphor. In T. R. Besold, M. Schorlemmer & A. Smaill (Eds.), *Computational creativity research: Towards creative machines* (pp. 217–242). Atlantis Press.

Bednarek, M. (2009). Emotion talk and emotional talk: Cognitive and discursive perspectives. *Language and Social Cognition: Expression of the Social Mind, 206*, 395–431.

Bledow, R., Rosing, K., & Frese, M. (2013). A dynamic perspective on affect and creativity. *Academy of Management Journal, 56*(2), 432–450.

Bozeman, B., & Feeney, M. K. (2014). *Rules and red tape: A prism for public administration theory and research.* Routledge.

Burgers, C., & Ahrens, K. (2020). Change in metaphorical framing: Metaphors of trade in 225 years of State of the Union addresses. *Applied Linguistics, 41*(2), 260–279.

Burrell, N. A., Buzzanell, P. M., & McMillan, J. J. (1992). Feminine tensions in conflict situations as revealed by metaphoric analyses. *Management Communication Quarterly, 6*(2), 115–149.

Cameron, L. (2003). *Metaphor in educational discourse.* Continuum.

Carter, R. (2015). *Language and creativity: The art of common talk* (2nd ed.). Routledge.
Cassell, C., & Bishop, V. (2019). Qualitative data analysis: Exploring themes, metaphors and stories. *European Management Review, 16*(1), 195–207.
Cassell, C., & Lee, B. (2012). Driving, steering, leading, and defending: Journey and warfare metaphors of change agency in trade union learning initiatives. *The Journal of Applied Behavioral Science, 48*(2), 248–271.
Chun, Y. H., & Rainey, H. G. (2006). Consequences of goal ambiguity in public organizations. In G. A. Boyne, K. J. Meier, L. J. O'Toole, Jr., & R. M. Walker. (Eds.), *Public Service Performance* (pp. 92–112). Cambridge University Press.
Colston, H. L., & Gibbs, R. W. (2021). Figurative language communicates directly because it precisely demonstrates what we mean. *Canadian Journal of Experimental Psychology/Revue Canadienne de Psychologie Expérimentale, 75*(2), 228–233. https://doi.org/10.1037/cep0000254
Deignan, A., Littlemore, J., & Semino, E. (2013). *Figurative language, genre and register*. Cambridge University Press.
Fainsilber, L., & Ortony, A. (1987). Metaphorical uses of language in the expression of emotions. *Metaphor and Symbol, 2*(4), 239–250.
Fuoli, M., Littlemore, J., & Turner, S. (2021). Sunken Ships and Screaming Banshees: Metaphor and evaluation in film reviews. *English Language and Linguistics, 26*(1), 75–103.
Gibbs Jr, R. W. (1994). *The poetics of mind: Figurative thought, language, and understanding*. Cambridge University Press.
Gibbs Jr, R. W. (2019). Metaphor as dynamical–ecological performance. *Metaphor and Symbol, 34*(1), 33–44.
Gibbs Jr, R. W. (2022). *The nature of figurative language*. Presented at the Figurative Thought and Language Conference, Poznan, Poland.
Gibson, C. B., & Zellmer-Bruhn, M. E. (2001). Metaphors and meaning: An intercultural analysis of the concept of teamwork. *Administrative Science Quarterly, 46*(2), 274–303.
Hendricks, R. K., Demjén, Z., Semino, E., & Boroditsky, L. (2018). Emotional implications of metaphor: Consequences of metaphor framing for mindset about cancer. *Metaphor and Symbol, 33*(4), 267–279.
Heracleous, L., & Jacobs, C. D. (2011). *Crafting strategy: Embodied metaphors in practice*. Cambridge University Press.
Hitchner, S., Schelhas, J., & Brosius, J. P. (2016). Snake oil, silver buckshot, and people who hate us: Metaphors and conventional discourses of wood-based bioenergy in the rural Southeastern United States. *Human Organization, 75*(3), 204–217.
Hood, S., & Martin, J. (2005). Invoking attitude: The play of graduation in appraising discourse. In R. Hasan, C. M. I. M. Matthiessen & J. J. Webster (Eds.), *Continuing discourse on language: A functional perspective* (Vol. 2, pp. 739–764). Equinox.
Johnson, M. (2013). *The body in the mind: The bodily basis of meaning, imagination, and reason*. University of Chicago Press.
Lakoff, G., & Johnson, M. (1980). *Metaphors we live by*. University of Chicago Press.
Littlemore, J., Pérez-Sobrino, P., Houghton, D., Shi, J., & Winter, B. (2018). What makes a good metaphor? A cross-cultural study of computer-generated metaphor appreciation. *Metaphor and Symbol, 33*(2), 101–122. https://doi.org/10.1080/10926488.2018.1434944
Liu, F. (2018). Lexical metaphor as affiliative bond in newspaper editorials: A systemic functional linguistics perspective. *Functional Linguistics, 5*(1), 2.

MacCormac, E. R. (1986). Creative metaphors. *Metaphor and Symbol, 1*(3), 171–184.
Martin, J. R., & White, P. R. R. (2005). *The language of evaluation: Appraisal in English.* Palgrave Macmillan.
Moon, R. (1998). *Fixed expressions and idioms in English: A corpus-based approach.* Clarendon Press.
Morgan, G. (1998). *Images of organization: The executive edition.* Sage.
Morgan, G. (2016). Commentary: Beyond Morgan's eight metaphors. *Human Relations, 69*(4), 1029–1042.
Musch, J., & Klauer, K. C. (2003). *The psychology of evaluation: Affective processes in cognition and emotion.* Psychology Press.
Nijstad, B. A., De Dreu, C. K., Rietzschel, E. F., & Baas, M. (2010). The dual pathway to creativity model: Creative ideation as a function of flexibility and persistence. *European Review of Social Psychology, 21*(1), 34–77.
Ortony, A., & Fainsilber, L. (1987). The role of metaphors in descriptions of emotions. In Y. Wilks (Ed.), *Theoretical issues in natural language processing* (pp. 178–182). Lawrence Erlbaum.
Partington, A. (1998). *Patterns and meanings.* John Benjamins.
Pérez-Sobrino, P., Semino, E., Ibarretxe-Antuñano, I., Koller, V., & Olza, I. (2021). Acting like a hedgehog in times of pandemic: Metaphorical creativity in the #ReframeCovid collection. *Metaphor and Symbol, 37*(2), 127–139.
Rhodes, R. A. (2007). Understanding governance: Ten years on. *Organization Studies, 28*(8), 1243–1264.
Richardson, J., & McKenna, S. (2000). Metaphorical "types" and human resource management: Self-selecting expatriates. *Industrial and Commercial Training, 32*(6), 209–229.
Rozin, P., & Royzman, E. B. (2001). Negativity bias, negativity dominance, and contagion. *Personality and Social Psychology Review, 5*(4), 296–320.
Runco, M. A., & Jaeger, G. J. (2012). The standard definition of creativity. *Creativity Research Journal, 24*(1), 92–96.
Russ, S. W. (2013). *Affect and creativity: The role of affect and play in the creative process.* Routledge.
Semino, E. (2008). *Metaphor in discourse.* Cambridge University Press.
Simon-Vandenbergen, A.-M. (2003). Lexical metaphor and interpersonal meaning. In A.-M. Simon- Vandenbergen, M. Taverniers & L. Ravelli (Eds.), *Amsterdam studies in the theory and history of linguistic science* (Vol. 4, pp. 223–256) Amsterdam: John Benjamins.
Thibodeau, P. H., Hendricks, R. K., & Boroditsky, L. (2017). How linguistic metaphor scaffolds reasoning. *Trends in Cognitive Sciences, 21*(11), 852–863.
Tosey, P., Lawley, J., & Meese, R. (2014). Eliciting metaphor through C lean language: An innovation in qualitative research. *British Journal of Management, 25*(3), 629–646.
Tracy, S. J., Lutgen-Sandvik, P., & Alberts, J. K. (2006). Nightmares, demons, and slaves: Exploring the painful metaphors of workplace bullying. *Management Communication Quarterly, 20*(2), 148–185.
Tsoukas, H. (1993). Analogical reasoning and knowledge generation in organization theory. *Organization Studies, 14*(3), 323–346.
Turner, S. L. (2014). *The development of metaphoric competence in French and Japanese learners of English.* Unpublished PhD Thesis, University of Birmingham.

Tyler, M., & Wilkinson, A. (2007). The tyranny of corporate slenderness: Corporate anorexia' as a metaphor for our age. *Work, Employment and Society, 21*(3), 537–549.

Vaara, E., Tienari, J., & Säntti, R. (2003). The international match: Metaphors as vehicles of social identity-building in cross-border mergers. *Human Relations, 56*(4), 419–451.

Werkmann Horvat, A. W., Bolognesi, M., Littlemore, J., & Barnden, J. (2022). Comprehension of different types of novel metaphors in monolinguals and multilinguals. *Language and Cognition, 14*(3), 1–36.

Werkmann Horvat, A., Bolognesi, M., & Kohl, K. (2021). Creativity is a toaster: Experimental evidence on how multilinguals process novel metaphors. *Applied Linguistics, 42*(5), 823–847.

Williams-Whitney, D., Mio, J. S., & Whitney, P. (1992). Metaphor production in creative writing. *Journal of Psycholinguistic Research, 21*(6), 497–509.

Winter, B. (2019). *Sensory linguistics: Language, perception and metaphor*. John Benjamins Publishing Company.

2 'I'm surprised anybody can hear anything going on for the crashing of all of these elephants in the room'

Methodology and taxonomy of creative metaphor types

Introduction

In this chapter, we describe the methodology employed in the study. We provide details of the participants and the interview procedure, the metaphor identification procedure that was employed, our approach to the identification of creative metaphor, and the process that we used to identify positive and negative evaluation. The bulk of the chapter is given over to our taxonomy of creative metaphor types. Although this is an important part of the methodology, it also constitutes a key contribution of our study as it provides a nuanced and fine-grained account of the ways that metaphor is used creatively in authentic discourse.

Participants and interview procedure

In order to answer our research questions, we analysed the language used in interviews with 31 senior current (N = 26) and former (N = 5) UK Civil Servants. The interviews were conducted by one of the authors (Tuck) between October 2013 and September 2014. The interviews were conducted in person with the exception of one interview which was conducted by telephone. They took place at the place of work of the interviewees with the exception of two interviewees who had left the Civil Service. These interviews took place in coffee shops. All interviews were recorded and lasted between 24 and 113 minutes. The average length of an interview was 58 minutes. In the interviews, participants were invited to reflect on their experience of working in the Civil Service, and on the ways in which performance is measured in that workplace. The interviews were transcribed and the transcripts were uploaded into NVivo, a qualitative research package which is used to assist in data organisation, annotation and categorisation.

Procedure used for the identification of metaphor

The transcripts of the interviews were coded in NVivo for metaphor by two of the authors (Littlemore and Turner). In order to decide whether an utterance

DOI: 10.4324/9781003262862-2

was metaphorical or not, we adopted Cameron and Maslen's (2010) approach to metaphor identification, which classifies metaphor at the level of the meaning unit rather than only focusing on individual lexical items. This allows the researcher to capture particular experiences that are described through metaphor. According to Cameron and Maslen (2010, 102–103), 'linguistic metaphor can be operationalized [...] through identifying words or phrases that can be justified as somehow anomalous, incongruous or "alien" in the on-going discourse, but that can be made sense of through a transfer of meaning in the context'. Following Steen et al. (2010), this transfer of meaning was coded as metaphor when it involved a comparison with a more basic sense. This basic sense could be more concrete, or more strongly related to a physical or bodily action to the contextual meaning. If the phrase had more basic current–contemporary meaning in other contexts than the given context, and the contextual meaning contrasted with the basic meaning but could be understood in comparison with it, it was marked as metaphorical. Our method departed from Steen et al.'s method in that we allowed word class boundaries to be crossed. In the majority of cases, the presence of a more basic sense was clear to the coders. In cases where the coders were unsure whether there was a more basic sense, the MacMillan and Longman Learners' Dictionaries were consulted.

Consider, for example, the following utterance:

I thought they'd spit me out after about a year and a half

Here, the contextual meaning of the string 'spit me out' involves notions of sudden and violent 'rejection'. This meaning is identified through a process of comparison with the physical act of spitting out food. There is a clear comparison that can be drawn between a contextual sense and a more basic sense, and the string was therefore coded as metaphorical.

Metaphorical strings could be realised through a wide range of expressions of varying length and complexity and belonging to any word class. Text spans of any length were identified as a single metaphor if they were coherent. For example, the following phrase was counted as a single metaphor because the notion of 'excising' is coherent with the idea of 'poison' and would not make sense without it:

We'd excised an awful lot of poison

Each metaphor was classified into an over-arching category following Steen (1999). The ten categories that we identified are shown in Table 2.1.

In some cases, metaphors were part of more than one category. For example:

They run around fielding what it is that [he/she's] doing, and [he/she] just focuses on what it is that [he/she's] doing.

Table 2.1 The categories of metaphor with examples

Metaphor Category	Example
Eating and food	I thought they'd spit me out after about a year and a half
Family, upbringing and the home	We were baby, baby people I think sometimes people ultimately grow up in a stream in an organisation
Fighting, war and physical attack, military	These are not final wars, they're a series of battles
Health and injury	we'd excised an awful lot of poison
Journeys and/or movement from one place to another	The journey we're on here is a really hard journey, and will we ever get there?
Other types of movement that do not refer to journeys; constraints to movement	making space to get up the learning curve
Machinery, industry and manual labour	I'm not pressing the right levers
Sport and ludic pastimes	you'd lost some matches as well as won
Nature and the natural world	The sharks are loitering
Actions and experiences not included in other categories	I'll be in hot water

This was coded as involving both 'sport and ludic pastimes' and 'other types of movement that do not refer to journeys, and constraints to movement'.

The two coders began by working jointly on the first four transcripts in order to define and agree on the procedure used for metaphor identification and the categorisation scheme. They then coded four further transcripts each, independently, using the procedure that they had developed. They then read through each other's coding and identified potential sources of disagreement with respect to (a) the metaphoricity of a particular item, (b) whether or not an item should be categorised as a single metaphor or as two metaphors, and (c) the category within which it should be included. These potential sources of disagreement were then discussed at length and resolved. In some cases, this led to the development of a new category. When this occurred a search was conducted of the previously coded transcripts in order to identify any items that would be better suited to the newly created category. One area of overlap that posed particular challenges was the interface between 'sport and ludic pastimes' and 'fighting' as both categories could be evoked by references to competition or even fighting. Our discussion led to a tight set of criteria for inclusion in the 'sport of ludic pastimes' category that required specific use of vocabulary that was unambiguously related to sport (e.g. 'ball', 'hurdle', 'swim', or 'track'). An example of a new category that was created during this second stage of the coding process was 'other types of movement that do not refer to journeys, and constraints to movement'. This category was created as it helped us to disambiguate metaphorical 'journeys' from other types of metaphorical movement. After the coders had completed their lengthy discussion of the coding to date, the coders coded five further transcripts each, met again to discuss ambiguous cases, and then repeated the procedure for the remaining ten transcripts. By the end of the procedure, each of the transcripts had been coded by one of the coders, the coding had been carefully checked by the second coder and all potentially ambiguous cases discussed.

Procedure used for the identification of creative uses of metaphor and taxonomy of creative uses of metaphor

After the metaphors had been identified, they were then coded for whether or they could be considered to constitute 'creative uses of metaphor'. In order to identify creative uses of metaphor, we first ruled out all examples of metaphor use with which the two researchers were familiar. These were labelled 'conventional'. In order to establish whether the remaining uses could be categorised as 'creative', we searched for instances in the British National Corpus (the BNC) and on the web. If no instances were found, we then attempted to classify the metaphorical expression according to the type of creativity that it involved. The categories of creative metaphor use emerged during the course of the analysis. As a starting point, we used a taxonomy of creative uses of metaphor that we proposed in earlier work on the use of metaphor in film reviews (Fuoli et al., 2021). Nearly all of the creative uses of metaphor identified in this study fell into categories from that taxonomy, but as we will see below, one of them did not, thus highlighting the role played by genre and register in shaping metaphor use (Deignan et al., 2013).

Through this procedure, we identified as 'creative' all uses of metaphor including those that brought together two domains of experience that are not normally compared (for example, *soapy sponges* and *challenges*). We also included cases where the two domains of experience are conventionally compared but where the speaker was using these conventional comparisons in unconventional ways. Note here that we use the term 'creative uses of metaphor' rather than simply 'creative metaphor'. At the beginning of our analysis, we had sought to distinguish between 'creative metaphor' (which involve the juxtaposition of two previously unrelated entities) and 'creative uses of metaphor', which involve forms of language play that involve metaphor. However, in performing our analysis, it became apparent that this was a highly artificial distinction as there are no new juxtapositions that do not draw on an existing mapping at some level, and all creative uses of metaphor involve a degree of 'language play' (Cook, 2000).

The procedure for dividing up the work was identical to that employed for the metaphor identification task. That is to say, the two coders first worked together on four transcripts, then worked separately and came together to discuss small sets of transcripts until all the coding had been completed. Here we present the different ways in which the participants made creative use of metaphor. A single instance of creative metaphor use could (and often did) fall into more than one of these categories.

Creating a 'new' metaphorical mapping

Some of the creative uses of metaphor in our data appeared, at least at first sight, to involve the creation of new mappings (i.e. relationships between two previously unrelated concepts). These involved entities being talked about in terms of entities that are not normally used to describe them. At first sight, these examples would appear to meet the criteria to allow them to be described as 'novel' metaphor, as discussed in Chapter 1.

The first example of one such metaphor is the following, where the speaker describes the overall picture or goal of the project that he is leading as being like the picture of a completed jigsaw that can be found on the lid of the box:

> *How do you explain to people what this jigsaw box lid looks like that this is one piece of, and then keep taking people back to the jigsaw box lid?*

At first sight this appears to be a highly novel mapping, as references to jigsaw box lids are not usually made in relation to project management. However, on closer inspection, the metaphor can be seen to draw on the conventional metaphorical idea of the pieces of a jigsaw being put together to make a whole. The novelty of the metaphor lies in the *focus of attention*, i.e. it focuses not on the jigsaw itself, but on the picture on the lid of the box, which represents the ideal end product. The speaker also appears to be making an oblique reference to the idea of focusing on the 'big picture' and a listener may draw on this expression, or at least the ideas that it represents, in order to make sense of what he is saying.

The second example of a creative metaphor that appears to involve the creation of a new mapping is that which was used in the opening sections of this book:

> *My role here [is]a bit like an It's a Knockout game. I'm sort of running on this soapy conveyor belt with people throwing wet sponges at me and I've got this sodding great elastic band attached to my back. [...] What are the sponges? The Treasury has quite a few sponges*

Here the speaker is creating what appears to be a highly novel mapping between work in the Civil Service and participating in an 'It's a Knockout' championship. As we saw in Chapter 1, by alluding to this programme, he is able to convey a number of evaluations of his current position, namely that although the goal may ultimately be worthwhile, the day-to-day challenge is virtually impossible, all sorts of impediments are thrown in his way, he feels frustrated, and feels as if he is deliberately being set up to fail and to look ridiculous. At first sight, this comparison, along with its entailments of feeling like he is on a soapy conveyor belt, with people throwing wet sponges at him, appears to be highly unconventional. Work in the Civil Service is not normally described in these terms, and the image that it conveys is highly engaging. However, here too, there are oblique references to more conventional metaphorical relationships. For example, it is not unconventional to refer to work as a form of play or competition, and the reference to the conveyor belt draws on the conceptual metaphor whereby progress is talked about in terms of forward movement through space, and where impediments to progress are described as 'holding people back'. The sponges that are being thrown at him appear to represent criticisms that are being made of his ability, and the idea of criticisms being projectiles that are thrown at people is again highly conventional. What is new here is the projectiles are in fact wet sponges; they do not do any real harm, but they are inconvenient and make him look ridiculous. Therefore, although the comparison is a novel one, it draws on a range of conventional metaphorical mappings, extending them in unconventional, and somewhat comedic ways.

A third example of a creative metaphor that appears to involve a new metaphorical mapping, is the use of the term 'organ rejection' by one of the interviews to describe the process of being excluded from one of the Civil Service Departments:

> *You have to understand the nature of the beast in order to make a difference. And if you can't do that then you won't make it. Someone described it to me [...] as <u>organ rejection</u>, which is quite graphic but I can see what they mean. So fortunately I wasn't rejected.*

Here, the comparison between the idea of not being accepted by a particular department and the experience of 'organ rejection' certainly appears to be new. However, this expression extends a relatively conventional metaphor whereby an organisation is seen as a human body and members of that organisation are seen as parts of the body.

A similar example, which also involves references to toys and games, is the following, where the speaker compares running a department to playing with a toy train set:

> *You might get paid more, <u>you might have a smaller train set but you get to use the controls</u> rather than just be a – can't quite follow that analogy, but...*

Drawing a comparison between running a Civil Service department and playing with a toy train set appears to be novel, but again, it draws on a conventional metaphorical mapping between work and play. The expression is also analogous to the idea of being 'a big fish in a small pond' as it expresses the idea that it may sometimes be preferable to work for a smaller organisation than a larger and possibly more prestigious organisation, as one can have power and respect within such an organisation. Once again, although the metaphorical comparison appears to be novel at first sight, it is reminiscent of conventional metaphors through extension and analogy.

Examples such as these call into doubt the idea that a metaphorical expression can ever be described as being entirely 'new'. In order to find meaning in a creative metaphor, the reader or listener will always, ultimately, need to draw on some kind of underlying conventional metaphor, even if this process takes place at a very high level of abstraction. In other words, in order to be understandable, all creative products need to have a baseline of conventionality which is then manipulated in creative ways. This baseline may not be determined by the author or the creator of the product, but it needs to be perceived by the reader or the hearer at some level. For metaphorical expressions, this conventional baseline is most likely to take the form of a conceptual metaphor. Within Conceptual Metaphor Theory, Lakoff and Turner (2009) suggest several ways in which conceptual metaphors can be used creatively. These include 'extension' (which involves exploiting a normally unused element of the source domain of a conventional metaphorical mapping); 'elaboration' (which involves using the source domain of a conventional conceptual metaphor in an unusual way); 'combination' (which involves bringing together two conventional conceptual metaphors); and 'questioning' (which involves explicitly calling into doubt the appropriateness of a conventional conceptual metaphor). At a higher level of abstraction, we have primary metaphors (Grady, 1997) and arguably, over-arching ontological and conduit metaphors (Lakoff & Johnson, 1980). Completely new mappings would be impossible to understand without drawing at least in part on an existing metaphorical mapping. However, the mappings that underpin creative uses of metaphor vary according to their level of abstraction.

Introducing more detail into a conventional metaphorical expression or mapping

A particularly productive category of creative metaphor in our data involved the introduction of more detail into a conventional metaphorical expression. We found that the metaphors that were extended in this way varied considerably in their degree of specificity. In the first example, the speaker takes a highly specific metaphorical idiom, the idea of there being 'an elephant in the room', and develops it in a number of creative ways. The basic meaning of the expression is that there is an obvious problem or difficulty that is being deliberately ignored. Here, a participant takes this expression and extends it:

> *I don't like elephants in the room that nobody talks about – and I realised very quickly that that was deeply uncomfortable for the Civil Service.*

There are so many elephants in the room in a classic Civil Service meeting. I'm surprised anybody can hear anything going on for the crashing of all of these elephants in the room.

I'm somebody who will not ignore the elephant in the room. I might decide that this isn't the board meeting to talk about the elephant, but certainly as a non-executive director, my value set, I don't believe that any director – executive or non-executive – should be ignoring elephants in the room because that's not what you're paid for.

I pointed out that there was at least a grey shape in the corner and wouldn't it be an idea to talk about it?

He doesn't ever talk about the elephant in the room. My suspicion is that [NAME] doesn't even acknowledge grey.

This speaker begins by developing the idea of there being an elephant in the room by referring to the idea that there are multiple elephants in the room and by drawing attention to the noise that all these elephants might be making. He does this to emphasise the extent to which he perceives this to be an issue in the Civil Service. He then emphasises the importance of not ignoring the elephants in the room. Finally, after having established the elephants in the room as being a major problem, he refers to them metonymically by recounting an anecdote where he attempted to encourage colleagues to notice the 'grey shape in the corner' and referring to the fact that his colleague 'doesn't even acknowledge grey'. By using these examples, he is able to express a strong negative evaluation of the behaviour of his colleagues. Some of these examples also shade into hyperbole, which we discuss in the next section.

In some instances, the introduction of more detail into the conventional metaphor involved expressing the 'flip side' of a metaphorical scenario. We can see an example of this in the following utterance:

You're frozen out. So <u>you can be unfrozen back in</u>.

Here, the speaker takes the idiomatic expression of being 'frozen out' which refers to the idea that one might be excluded from a particular group, and argues that one can kind of be 'defrosted' or 'thawed', and let back into the group. Although this is a creative use of metaphor, it draws on the conventional idea of relationships 'thawing', although he uses alternative vocabulary.

A third example of a metaphor in this category is the following utterance, where the speaker takes the idea of being on a merry-go-round, which is a fairly conventional metaphor to represent the idea of working together in a somewhat mindless way, but he extends it to talk about spinning off the merry-go-round to refer to the idea of being rejected from the Civil Service or leaving it rapidly because for some reason they cannot cope or find themselves unsuited to the Civil Service working environment, and return to work in the private sector:

> So I suppose, *as people rotate round, some will spin off the merry-go-round and shoot off* back to the private sector.

Other examples of metaphors within this category include the following:

> So *if somebody's invented the wheel, just go and get the wheel*: you don't need to do it yourself.

> It's amazing how much, *by putting a few deposits in the favour bank early on in your career, you can withdraw quite a lot later on.*

> What they do is they exploit them by *dangling a very interesting carrot.*

The first of these expressions draws on (and extends) the metaphor of 'reinventing the wheel', which refers to the act of pointlessly recreating an object of an idea that has already been created or proposed. The second draws on (and extends) the metaphor of 'building up a favour bank', which expresses the idea that if one helps others, they are likely to feel indebted and help out in return. The third refers to the idea of dangling a carrot to tempt someone to do something that they may not otherwise want to do, but here it is not only a carrot, but a very interesting carrot.

In the example below, the speaker uses the idiom 'getting into the meat' which refers to the main or most important part of something, but he then extends it to refer to those aspects that are not the meat itself but are perhaps more superficial and pleasant than the 'meat' itself:

> But we're not into the meat, if you like. We're still cutting through the stuff that is nice to have here.

Some creative extensions of existing metaphors worked at a much more abstract, conceptual level than those mentioned so far. The conventional metaphor was not a specific metaphorical expression (such as 'the elephant in the room'), but rather a more general 'conceptual' metaphor, of the kind listed by Lakoff and Johnson (1980). This kind of creativity is akin to what Lakoff and Turner might describe as 'extension'. We are not making any claims here about whether the metaphors were actually being consciously or subconsciously drawn on by the speakers. Rather, we are talking about a higher level of abstraction at which metaphorical creativity can be identified. In our original taxonomy proposed in Fuoli et al. (2021), we did not draw attention to the different levels at which the creative extension of a metaphor can take place. However, we believe that it is an interesting theoretical consideration as it draws attention to the different levels at which creativity can manifest.

In the remaining part of this section, we provide examples of creative uses of metaphor where the creative extension process appears to have taken place at a more conceptual level. The first set of examples demonstrate extensions of conceptual metaphors involving spatial/orientation mapping:

... *words which sit <u>above and sort of slightly round the edge</u> of leadership*

You're very much in the business, not in that sort of <u>gilded cage of the centre</u>.

I was saying to a colleague of mine, it feels like <u>there's a secret door somewhere and you're not able to get through it.</u>

So I suppose, <u>as people rotate round, some will spin off the merry-go-round and shoot off</u> back to the private sector.

All of these metaphors involve bringing together previously un-combined elements, and none of them can be found in English language corpora. However, underpinning all of them is the idea that they extend physical spatial or orientation qualities to more abstract contexts. The first example draws on metaphorical ideas involving location as illustrated in the underlined segments. The second example is interesting as the speaker appears to be making a contrast between two different locations. The idea that one might be 'in the business' is a conventional way of referring to the fact that one is involved in the day-to-day running of the business. But then the speaker goes on to comment that they are not 'in that sort of gilded cage in the centre'. This evokes an image of a gilded cage sitting at the centre of the activity, with the actual business taking place around the edges of the cage. It is a highly original image but draws on a basic metaphorical mapping between physical space and virtual space.

In the third example, the idea of a 'secret door' suggests that there may be metaphorical 'places' (i.e. ways of being, thinking etc.) that one has to be 'in the know' to find out about. Again, this is a previously unattested metaphorical idea, but it can be traced to the idea of movement through space. The idea of movement through space being mapped into a more abstract domain is also present in the fifth example, where people are seen to 'shoot off' back to the private sector as they get thrown off the merry-go-round.

Some of the examples of creative uses of metaphor within this category involved extensions of the conduit metaphor. According to this conceptual metaphor, human communication and exchanges of ideas are conceptualised as exchanges of physical objects. In the following example, the speaker extends this idea to suggest that the central government is throwing the less interesting aspects of the work at local government:

Government keeps <u>lobbing bits of uninteresting stuff</u> towards local government

Other examples of creative uses of metaphor that involved extensions of one or more conceptual metaphor are following:

24   *Methodology and creative metaphor taxonomy*

> Things keep <u>popping in</u> from the outside world and <u>poking you on the nose</u>
>
> It would just be <u>a ramble through [NAME]'s head</u>

Both of these examples can be traced to the idea of the container metaphor, and the second example combines this with a journey metaphor, but here the journey has become somewhat lacking in direction and is combined with the metonym whereby a person's head represents their thoughts. We discuss this kind of creativity in more detail below. In some cases, the creative extensions of existing metaphor involved hyperbole. We can see an example of this in the following expression:

> We're like <u>in kindergarten</u> [...] <u>We're still on liquids; I'm not sure we've got to solid foods yet</u>.

Here, the speaker draws on the metaphor of Civil Servants being treated and behaving like children, but he takes it right back to very early childhood, by saying that they are not on solid foods yet (i.e. referring to the first few months of life).

Alluding to, appropriating and/or recontextualising an idiom or a well-known phrase

Some creative uses of metaphor involved the use of well-known metaphorical phrases from literature or films where one word was substituted with a word that was relevant to the context at hand. Here is an example which involves an adaptation of a quote from William Shakespeare:

> ... grow up in Defence and have Finance thrust upon you, as it were

This is a reference to the extract 'Some are born great, some achieve greatness, and some have greatness thrust upon them', which appears in Act II Scene 5 of Twelfth Night. In the play, the quote constitutes part of a joke. It is an extract from a letter that a noble lady, Olivia allegedly wrote to Malvolio, one of her servants. He reads it out loud, thinking that Olivia is in love with him and that she would like him to better himself. He is unaware of the fact that the letter has in fact been written by his fellow servants in an effort to play a joke on him. It encourages him to do the very things that annoy his mistress the most.

In our study, the speaker uses it to express the idea that people are generally reluctant to work in the Finance department and that they are generally given very little choice about working there. The fact that it parallels the 'greatness' in the quote from Shakespeare where it was mentioned in an ironic way as part of a practical joke suggests that he does not necessarily think that working in France is a good thing, although it may help one's career prospects.

Altering the valence of a conventional metaphor

At times, creative uses of metaphor involved taking a conventional metaphor and changing its valence so that things that are normally talked about in a positive light are viewed negatively, or vice versa. We can see an example of this in the following utterance:

> *If somebody's not even <u>in the headlights of the head-hunters</u>, those people will probably not be making the changes.*

This utterance draws on the conventional metaphorical idea of being 'a rabbit/deer in headlights', which expresses the idea that one is so nervous, they are unable to move or to speak. It draws on the idea that one feels like prey and is rendered immobile. Here however, the headlights are those of the 'head-hunters' (i.e. people who identify and approach suitable candidates employed elsewhere to fill business positions), so the meaning here is positive; normally, one would want to find oneself in the headlights of the head-hunters, as it suggests that the head-hunters have 'set their sights' on you and that they may therefore be considering offering you a job. This example is rendered particularly interesting by the fact that the older, more basic sense of the term 'head-hunter' refers to someone who collects the heads of dead enemies as trophies, so the original meaning of the expression is inherently negative. It may have been the case that the speaker was alluding to this idea (albeit subconsciously). Taking all of this information together, the idea of being 'in the headlights of the head-hunters' has mixed and ambiguous polarity, which contributes to its overall creative feel.

A second example of a creative use of metaphor that involves altering the valence of a conventional metaphorical idea is the following utterance, which was used by a participant to refer to progression and promotion within the Civil Service:

> *... further up the pile you go*

At first sight, this appears to be a positive expression, as it refers to the idea of moving up through the hierarchy. However, the use of the word 'pile' here jars slightly with this idea as 'piles' are normally used to refer to non-human objects which means that 'being in a pile' is somewhat depersonalising. Being in a pile is likely to make one feel worthless and lacking in individuality. It also evokes negative expressions such as 'a pile of shit' or 'being at the bottom of the pile'.

Altering the tense or part of speech of a conventional metaphor

Another way of using metaphor in a creative way involved altering the tense or the part of speech that was used in a conventional metaphor. This also included turning countable entities into uncountable ones. For example, the countable noun 'spark' is conventionally used in English to refer to intelligence ('a bright spark') but in the following example, it is used as an uncountable noun and in a relatively passive construction:

> There was a *less tangible sense of spark*

It is also worth noting that in this example the idea of a spark is also talked about as if it were possible to experience it in a sensory way, as it is talked about as being 'less tangible'.

Introducing a new collocation

At times, participants made creative use of metaphor by introducing a new collocation. In the following example, the speaker uses the word 'up' after 'excel'. A more conventional collocation here would be 'excel in':

> ... *excel up each of those channels*

This example is talked about in more detail below.

Using a metaphor to talk about something that it's not usually used to talk about

Some creative uses of metaphor involved the use of a conventional metaphor to talk about something that it is not normally used to refer to. Interestingly, in our data, all of the examples that fell into this category involved depersonalisation. In the following examples, people are talked about as if they are industrial products or entities that can be transferred between individuals:

> So you're not the *primary output*, as it were

> ... *moved over here for a year's loan*

It is relatively conventional in English to talk about productivity in very physical terms, so even intangible results of labour can be referred to as 'products' or 'outputs'. However, it is rare to talk about people in this way. In the first example above, an employee is described as an 'output' (and not even a primary one!) and in the second example, an employee is 'loaned' to another department, as if they were an object such as a pen or a photocopier. These kinds of metaphors may have been intended to provide a somewhat critical comment on an aspect of Civil Service culture, where employees might be viewed as inanimate 'objects' that can be easily replaced.

Employing a metaphor that interacts with metonymy in a novel way

Some creative uses of metaphor involved interactions with metonymy. This could be done in different ways. In the first example, there is a PART-WHOLE metonymic relationship at play, as the person is used to refer to their skills, the work that would be done by that person, and the time that they are contracted to work. However, this is re-literalised to refer specifically to the body and its parts. This allows for a second part-whole metonymic relationship where an arm and a leg are used to represent the fact that they are not 100% available. It is also reminiscent of the idiomatic expression 'costs an arm and a leg'.

> *All the talent work I've been doing myself with the help of someone in HMRC who's been seconded to me for ten per cent of their time. So again, <u>it's a little bit of an arm and a leg rather than a whole person</u>.*

Some theories of metonymy see it as sitting between metaphor and literal meaning (see Paprotté & Dirven, 1985). Here we have an example of a creative manipulation of this idea:

> *I think in reality they wouldn't be <u>in that marketplace</u> looking for somebody in that sort of area.*

In this example, the conventional term is 'to be in the market' whereas here it is adjusted to 'marketplace' which evokes a physical space and is therefore more literal.

Sometimes creative combinations of metaphor and metonymy involved allusions to popular culture. We can see this in the following example:

> *I mean, I joined banking when it was <u>Captain Mainwaring territory</u> back in the seventies, and in the light of it I've seen big bang, globalisation, internationalisation and everything.*

Captain Mainwaring was one of the central characters in a BBC comedy programme from the 1970s entitled 'Dad's Army'. The programme was about a group of (mostly elderly) men, working for the 'Home Guard'. This was an organisation of local defence volunteers, consisting of men who were above or below the age of conscription or who were unfit or ineligible for front-line military service. The fictional Home Guard unit in the programme was very amateurish and continually messed things up; Captain Mainwaring was the head of the unit and in many ways the most ridiculous of all the characters. Therefore, by describing his work culture as being 'Captain Mainwaring territory', the speaker is saying that it was disorganised, amateurish, and a bit ridiculous. The word 'territory' in this utterance is of course a metaphor as it describes an abstract concept (the work culture) in terms of a more concrete one (territory). His use of the term 'territory' to describe the work culture also implies that the situation was in a state of flux, as 'territory' tends to change hands between enemy groups in a war setting.

In the following example, the speaker combines the metaphor 'ramble' with the metonymy 'head', which stands for the brain or thinking processes:

> *It's just been a <u>ramble through [NAME]'s head</u>*

This creative utterance inherits a degree of coherence from the idea that there can be 'patterns' or 'trains' of thought, that convey the idea of movement.

Combining two or more metaphors

Some creative uses of metaphor involved the combination of two or more metaphors that at first sight appear to be incompatible, but which become compatible in the metaphorical space. This incompatibility sometimes appeared to operate at the level of conceptual metaphor, as in the following examples, each of which combines an expression motivated by the GOOD IS UP conceptual metaphor with an expression motivated by the SOURCE PATH GOAL conceptual metaphor:

> *... <u>moving up</u> that sort of value-added journey*

> *... <u>excel up</u> each of those channels*

Each of these cases contains reference to movement, which would normally be in a general horizontal direction ('channels'; 'journey'), but here the direction of the 'journey' is orientated upwards through the use of the proposition 'up'. This makes the utterances appear marked and therefore more 'creative', as it forces the listener to shift their perspective from a horizontal one that is associated with journeys to a vertical one.

At other times, the incompatibility appears to be more at the linguistic level where two scenes were juxtaposed that would be incompatible in the physical world. We can see this in the following example:

> *... helping <u>guide this supertanker through the minefields</u> of Cabinet Office and Treasury*

In this example, there is an apparent incompatibility between a 'supertanker' and 'minefields', as supertankers operate on the sea, whereas one is more likely to consider a 'minefield' to be on land. However, in the metaphorical space, this potential discrepancy is overlooked, and the idea of driving something (hyperbolically) large through a minefield is all that is retained.

The metaphors in this section appear to bring together two apparently incompatible entities which is resonant of blending theory (Fauconnier &

Turner, 2008); they make sense in the context of the metaphor but would be unlikely to occur in the physical world.

Making use of strong, unlikely or unexpected personification

Some creative uses of metaphor involved strong, unlikely or unexpected uses of personification. We can see this in the following two examples:

> Central government keeps <u>throwing more grenades over the parapet</u> and screaming 'make more cuts, make more cuts'
>
> Things keep <u>popping in</u> from the outside world and poking <u>you on the nose</u>

In the first example, 'central government' is personified as someone (possibly a soldier) who is 'throwing grenades', whilst at the same time insisting that the Department 'makes more cuts'. The fact that the soldier is performing both of these apparently contradictory actions at once marks them out as someone who is irrational, unreasonable, and possibly quite childish. In the second example, unexpected events 'pop in from the outside' and 'poke [the protagonist] on the nose'. Again, these events are personified, and construed (possibly) as naughty, cheeky children or gremlins.

Making use of 'twice true' metaphor

Some creative uses of metaphor involved working with ideas that work on both a literal and a metaphorical level and which are therefore 'twice true' (Camp, 2006).

> I always try and think, you know, not just when I step into a job how I step into it, but how I'm going to step out. I sort of thought I might step out of my current job into being a divisional FD here, and that door's certainly not closed to me; I'd come back and do that, I think, when there's a vacancy. But I hope I don't step out to Botany Bay, which is where my predecessor's gone, but probably into an FD role somewhere, a government agency.

In this example, the speaker talks metaphorically about the idea of 'stepping into' and 'stepping out of' jobs. He then uses the word 'step' in a more literal (albeit hyperbolic) way to describe how his predecessor ended up in Botany Bay. Here the meaning of the word 'stepping' is closer to its literal sense as it refers to movement and travel. This provides a slightly humorous contrast with the more mundane, metaphorical uses of the word that appear at the beginning of the citation. We discuss the use of contrast in the following section.

Making use of contrast

In some cases, a conventional metaphor was used to provide a deliberate contrast with another metaphor. We can see an example of this in the following utterance:

> *I mean, the good policy generalist can become a different person overnight. They can move from being right-wing of Attila the Hun to being left of Karl Marx in their outlook.*

Here, extreme left-wing and extreme right-wing political views are being compared, with extreme metonymic exemplars of those views being provided in each case.

In other cases, the contrast was between the metaphor and the literal context in which it was being used:

> *Oh, it's [NAME]. Basically [NAME] is half empty all the time*

Here the speaker uses the conventional metaphor 'half empty' to suggest that Fred is a natural pessimist. It could relate to the idea (and corresponding expression) that if someone is a pessimist, they would see a half-full glass as 'half empty', or it could relate to the idea that if someone lacks energy or verve, they are 'running on empty' (i.e. their metaphorical petrol tank is empty). The 'half' here contrasts with the 'all' which is used in a more literal sense of 'all the time'.

Employing several of the above categories in combination

Some of the creative uses of metaphor involved employing several of the creative uses that have been listed above. We can see an example of this in the following utterance:

> *She did the traditional sort of chuck it all up in the air, so get all the deckchairs and throw them up in the air, cause chaos for a year and a half and then leave, and that's basically what she did.*

Here, the speaker is referring to a former Head of Department, who he believes to have been a poor, disorganised leader. Rather than planning carefully, he says that she simply 'chucked it all up in the air', which refers to a 'management style' where one has no plan in place whatsoever and simply 'chucks it all up in the air and see how it lands'. The idea of throwing things in the air and seeing how they land is often used to suggest that someone is bringing in large, and possibly unnecessary, changes without any sense of purpose or strategy. However, not only did she do this, but she also 'got all the deckchairs and threw them up in the air'. The fact that the manager is throwing deckchairs in the air is possibly an allusion to the idiomatic expression 'rearranging the deckchairs on the Titanic' which is sometimes used to refer to ineffectual and superficial behaviour in the face of an impending disaster.

Making use of extended analogies/metaphorical scenarios

In our data, we identified a category of creative uses of metaphor which was not present in our previous taxonomy. This category involved the use of extended analogies or metaphorical scenarios to evaluatively describe a complex set of behaviours. We can see an example of this in the following exchange:

> *[Interviewee] And he's the sort of manager who'll say 'bring me a pebble', and you go and find him a pebble. And he'll say, 'no, no, no, bigger', 'no, no, no, rounder', 'no, no, no, different'. And three weeks later he'll actually decide what he wanted was a half brick. He's a bit like that. And interesting, because he does his thinking in camera.*
>
> *[Interviewer] What do you mean by that?*
>
> *[Interviewee] In that he doesn't work out what he wants to do and then come to a decision and tell his subordinates. He spends a period of time testing ideas on his subordinates, having a dialogue with them about how something might be done, and he throws suggestions out expecting to be challenged and having that dialogue. And you either get that with [NAME] or you don't.*

Here we have not highlighted any of the expressions as being metaphorical as we consider the whole of the first utterance to be metaphorical as the manager in question is not literally asking for a pebble. However, the whole extended scenario demonstrates a particular management style in which the manager is using his subordinates' attempts to fulfil his first request to clarify for himself what he wanted in the first place. The exasperation the speaker feels is expressed not only through the futility of the actions described in the metaphor, but also through the use of repetition of the word 'no' in the hypothetical reported speech (Koester, 2014; Mayes, 1990). There is therefore a creative interplay between the chosen metaphor used and the way in which it is formulated linguistically which contributes to the evaluative power of the utterance.

The fact that this category of creative uses of metaphor was so noticeable in this dataset may reflect genre and register features of the data. The Civil Servants were being interviewed about their experiences and were being encouraged to go into detail on these. It is likely that they drew on these extended analogies and scenarios to put their personal experiences across in a way that would be understood by their interlocutors. Indeed, extended metaphors have been shown to be an important component of narratives in spoken discourse (Ritchie, 2010).

Procedure used for the identification of positive and negative evaluation

The metaphors were coded according to whether they performed a positive evaluation, a negative evaluation, a mixed/ambiguous evaluation, or no evaluation. A metaphor was coded as serving an evaluative function if, on the analyst's reading and interpretation of the text, they believed that it expressed a speaker's or another person's positive or negative emotions, attitudes, and judgments towards something or someone.

A metaphor was coded as performing positive evaluation if it conveyed a positive assessment of or emotion towards someone or something:

> *And in particular in Defence – and this is common, I think, in a lot of departments across Whitehall – it's moving up that sort of <u>value-added journey</u> [+ **evaluation**] of not simply thinking about the transactional underpinnings.*

A metaphor was coded as performing negative evaluation if a negative assessment of or emotion towards someone or something:

> *<u>I'm sort of running on this soapy conveyor belt with people throwing wet sponges at me and I've got this sodding great elastic band attached to my back</u> [- **evaluation**].*

A metaphor was coded as conveying mixed/ambiguous evaluation if the evaluation was both positive and negative:

> *I was <u>just holding a mirror up to the organisation</u>*

This utterance contains positive evaluation as the speaker was helping those in the organisation to get a better picture of how the organisation was working, but it also contains negative evaluation as some aspects of the organisation were not working well.

A metaphor was coded as performing no evaluation if there was no clear positive or negative evaluative content:

> *That's <u>a bit down the track</u>*

Here, the metaphor simply refers to future plans which are not being evaluated positively or negatively.

The identification of evaluation types was performed by a research assistant and verified by two of the authors (Littlemore and Turner).

Conclusion

In this chapter we have outlined the methodology used in the study. We have described our procedure for identifying metaphors and classifying them into different themes, our procedure for identifying creative metaphor, and our procedure for identifying positive and negative evaluation. We identified a range of creative uses of metaphor following Fuoli et al., (2021) but we added the new category of 'creative metaphorical scenarios', whose predominance we attribute to the genre of the dataset. We have suggested that, in order to do justice to the human role in producing 'creative metaphor' it is more appropriate to use the term 'creative use of metaphor' rather than simply 'creative metaphor'. We have seen that creative uses of metaphor can involve: the creation of an apparently 'new' metaphorical mapping (though an existing mapping can always be identified at some level); introducing more detail into a conventional mapping; combining metaphor with hyperbole; alluding to or recontextualising an idiom or a well-known phrase; altering the valence of a conventional metaphor; altering the tense or part of speech of a conventional metaphor; using a metaphor to talk about something that it's not usually used to talk about; employing a metaphor that interacts with metonymy in a novel way; combining two or more metaphors; making use of strong, unlikely, or unexpected personification; making use of extended analogies/metaphorical scenarios; making use of 'twice true' metaphors; or making use of contrast. A number of creative uses of metaphor involved combinations of these different strategies.

References

Cameron, L., & Maslen, R. (2010). *Metaphor analysis*. Equinox.
Camp, E. (2006). Contextualism, metaphor, and what is said. *Mind & Language, 21*(3), 280–309.
Cook, G. (2000). *Language play, language learning*. Oxford University Press.
Deignan, A., Littlemore, J., & Semino, E. (2013). *Figurative language, genre and register*. Cambridge University Press.
Fauconnier, G., & Turner, M. (2008). *The way we think: Conceptual blending and the mind's hidden complexities*. Basic Books.
Fuoli, M., Littlemore, J., & Turner, S. (2021). Sunken Ships and Screaming Banshees: Metaphor and evaluation in film reviews. *English Language and Linguistics, 26*(1), 75–103.
Grady, J. (1997). *Foundations of meaning: Primary metaphors and primary scenes*. PhD Dissertation, University of California at Berkley.
Koester, A. (2014). 'We'd be prepared to do something, like if you say...' hypothetical reported speech in business negotiations. *English for Specific Purposes, 36*, 35–46.

Lakoff, G., & Johnson, M. (1980). *Metaphors we live by*. University of Chicago Press.

Lakoff, G., & Turner, M. (2009). *More than cool reason: A field guide to poetic metaphor*. University of Chicago Press.

Mayes, P. (1990). Quotation in spoken English. *Studies in Language. International Journal Sponsored by the Foundation 'Foundations of Language,'* 14(2), 325–363.

Paprotté, W., & Dirven, R. (1985). *The ubiquity of metaphor: Metaphor in language and thought (Vol. 29)*. John Benjamins Publishing.

Ritchie, L. D. (2010). 'Everybody goes down': Metaphors, stories, and simulations in conversations. *Metaphor and Symbol*, 25(3), 123–143.

Steen, G., Dorst, A. G., Herrmann, J. B., Kaal, A., Krennmayr, T., & Pasma, T. (2010). *A method for linguistic metaphor identification*. Amsterdam: Benjamins.

3 'She did the traditional sort of chuck it all up in the air, so get all the deckchairs and throw them up in the air, cause chaos for a year and a half and then leave'

To what extent are creative metaphors used to perform evaluation and how do creative and conventional metaphors relate to one another?

Introduction

In this chapter we begin by presenting the responses to our three main research questions:

1. To what extent is metaphor used to express evaluation in conversations about work?
2. Is the use of metaphor more likely to be associated with positive or negative evaluation?
3. Do creative and conventional metaphor differ in terms of the extent to which they express (positive or negative) evaluation?

We then drill down into our data a little more and explore in more detail how exactly our participants used creative and conventional metaphor to evaluate their experiences of working in the Civil Service. We explore the ten categories of metaphor; discuss the extent to which each category was used creatively or conventionally to express positive, negative, or mixed/ambiguous evaluation; and conduct a qualitative analysis in order to show how the creative and conventional uses of metaphor within these categories related to one another. Our intention is to build up an overall picture of how creative and conventional metaphor was used to convey evaluation in conversations about the Civil Service workplace.

DOI: 10.4324/9781003262862-3

36 *Creative metaphors and evaluation*

To what extent is metaphor used to express evaluation in conversations about work? Is the use of metaphor more likely to be associated with positive or negative evaluation? And do creative and conventional metaphor differ in terms of the extent to which they express (positive or negative) evaluation?

In order to answer the first three research questions, we need to look at the relative tendencies of metaphor as a whole (and creative and conventional metaphor in particular) to perform positive evaluation, negative evaluation, mixed/ambiguous evaluation, or no evaluation. The findings from this part of the study can be found in Table 3.1.

We can see from Table 3.1 that the general trend was for metaphor to perform evaluation more often than it was used in non-evaluative contexts, and that it was more likely to perform negative evaluation than positive evaluation. However, this finding in itself does not tell us much as it could well be the case that the participants were providing negative evaluations of their workplace environments in general, regardless of whether they were using metaphor. What is interesting in this table are the differences between the columns in terms of both direction and magnitude. When we compare the column showing the extent to which creative metaphor was used to perform the different types of evaluation with the column showing how conventional metaphor was used to perform evaluation, we see that in comparison with conventional metaphor, creative metaphor was used relatively more often to perform evaluation than not χ^2 (1) 6.5544, $p < .05$. The evaluation performed by creative metaphor was also relatively more likely to be negative than the evaluation performed by conventional metaphor χ^2 (1) 6.0615, $p < .05$. Thus, in comparison to conventional metaphor, creative metaphor was proportionally more likely than conventional metaphor to perform evaluation in general,

Table 3.1 Number of creative and conventional metaphors used to perform positive, negative, and mixed/ambiguous evaluation

	Creative metaphor (fitting into any of the ten categories described above, but only counted once)		Conventional metaphor (fitting into any of the ten categories described above, but only counted once)		All metaphors	
	Raw	%	Raw	%	Raw	%
Positive evaluation	13	16.05	174	31.58	187	29.59
Negative evaluation	35	43.21	206	37.39	241	38.13
Mixed/ambiguous evaluation	31	38.27	107	19.42	138	21.84
Not clearly evaluative	2	2.47	64	11.62	66	10.44
Total	81	100	551	100	632	100

and negative evaluation in particular. When we factored mixed evaluation into the calculations, we also found that when metaphor was being used to evaluate, creative metaphor was proportionately more likely to perform *negative or mixed/ambiguous evaluation* than conventional metaphor χ^2 (1) 11.4131, $p < .05$.

The association between creative metaphor and negative evaluation contrasts with previous work that we have conducted on the use of metaphor to perform evaluation in a different genre (that of film reviews), where we found this not to be the case. The difference in findings might be explained in the following way: A key difference between the film review data and the Civil Service data is that in the film reviews, critics are talking about things that are external to themselves, whereas in the Civil Service data people are talking about their own personal experiences – it is the personal nature of the experiences that we think may drive this relationship between creativity and negativity. In Chapter 1, we discussed work showing that the experience of negative emotion drives the production of creative metaphors, and the results that we have here speak to an increased role for emotion when recounting personal experiences than when describing third-party experiences. They also provide insights into the ways in which different genres can affect the ways in which people use metaphor to express evaluation. Our findings therefore constitute a new contribution to our understanding of the relationship between metaphor and evaluation and genre.

Which metaphors were used to perform what kinds of evaluation, and how were they employed?

As explained in Chapter 2, metaphors were categorised into ten broad categories. In Table 3.2 we show the number of occurrences of each metaphor category across the dataset and the different types of evaluation that each category of metaphor was used to perform. As we can see in Table 3.2, all the categories relate to an area of human experience, relating to either physical experiences involving the body itself or human interactions with the wider world. This finding is in line with current thinking on metaphor as an embodied phenomenon through which 'people's subjective, felt experiences of their bodies in action provide part of the fundamental grounding for language and thought' (Gibbs, 2005, 9). This characteristic also extended to the creative metaphors identified in our dataset. This coheres with Okonski et al.'s (2020, 20) observation that creative metaphors emerge from 'very ordinary, yet still highly metaphorical, conceptualisations of mundane bodily experiences'.

It can be seen from Table 3.2 that the more general categories of movement and general 'action and experience' metaphors were the most common metaphor type, followed by fighting and war and manual labour and industry. The most negatively evaluative categories were health and injury,

Table 3.2 Metaphor categories and the types of evaluation that they performed[1]

	Positive evaluation		Negative evaluation		Mixed evaluation		Not clearly evaluative		Total	
	Raw	%	Raw	%	Raw	%	Raw	%	Raw	%
Family, upbringing, and the home	12	35.29	12	35.29	8	23.53	2	5.88	34	100
Eating and food	14	48.28	10	34.48	3	10.34	2	6.90	29	100
Fighting, war and physical attack, military	13	21.31	28	45.90	20	32.79	0	0.00	61	100
Sport and ludic pastimes	9	20.00	16	35.56	16	35.56	4	8.89	45	100
Health and injury	1	6.67	11	73.33	3	20.00	0	0.00	15	100
Machinery, industry, and manual labour	31	44.29	23	32.86	9	12.86	7	10.00	70	100
Types of movement that do not refer to journeys; constraints to movement	65	28.51	83	36.40	49	21.49	31	13.60	228	100
Journeys and/or movement from one place to another	15	48.39	7	22.58	8	25.81	1	3.23	31	100
Nature and the natural world	18	33.33	19	35.19	9	16.67	8	14.81	54	100
Actions and experiences not included in other categories	26	22.03	55	46.61	24	20.34	13	11.02	118	100

general actions and experiences, and fighting, war and physical attack and the military. This is unsurprising given the nature of some of these fields; it would be expected for metaphors related to illness and injury, or to war, to be used to serve negative evaluative functions. Interestingly, this table also demonstrates that metaphors in categories that may traditionally be thought of as positive, e.g. the family, or sport and games, in fact served a range of evaluative functions.

Turning to the different types of metaphor, we found that metaphors relating to health and injury, and fighting, war and physical attack and the military were relatively more likely to perform negative evaluation. This is unsurprising given the nature of these fields.

We now provide a qualitative exploration of the metaphors that were used in each of these categories, focusing on how they were used, both conventionally and creatively to describe and evaluate the implicit workplace cultures that are in operation within the British Civil Service.

Family, upbringing, and the home

Metaphors referring to family, upbringing, and the home were prevalent in our data. They tended to be used conventionally and were used to perform both positive and negative evaluation.

Many participants conceptualised their advancement through the Civil Service as 'growing up' in a 'family' environment:

> *I think sometimes people ultimately grow up in a stream in an organisation*

This idea of 'growing up' was also reflected in this example of a creative reappropriation of a well-known phrase discussed in Chapter 2:

> *...grow up in Defence and have Finance thrust upon you, as it were*

Advancing in the Civil Service is 'growing up', and therefore, those in the more junior positions are considered to be infants:

> *When we were baby, baby people, they stripped you down and built you back up, on the logic that unless you know yourself you certainly can't tell anybody else how to do anything, yes?*

Supporting the development of these members of staff therefore draws on a number of associated metaphors, all related to family, upbringing and the home:

> *How much of this do you need to spoon feed*

Table 3.3 Percentages of creative and conventional metaphors involving family, upbringing, and the home

Evaluation	Conventional Raw	%	Creative Raw	%	Total Raw	%
Positive evaluation	12	40.00	0	0.00	12	35.29
Negative evaluation	10	33.33	2	50.00	12	35.29
Mixed/ambiguous evaluation	6	20.00	2	50.00	8	23.53
Not clearly evaluative	2	6.67	0	0.00	2	5.88
TOTAL	30	100	4	100	34	100

Some of these move the focus from infancy into childhood and adolescence:

...but they've just been <u>schooled</u> in a culture

...do one's <u>homework</u> about the values of the team you're about to join

Metaphors related to family, upbringing and the home were mixed in terms of the valence of evaluation they performed, being used equally frequently for positive and negative evaluation and serving mixed-valence evaluative functions too. For example, while some family-related metaphors were positively valenced (e.g. the idea of *doing one's homework*, above), they could also be used cynically:

I mean, you get together <u>supervised by the grown-ups</u>.

Metaphorical conceptualisations of the Civil Service as a family were also used to present less positive aspects of the experience of working there, as we can see in the following examples. Here we have an example in which the parent–child relationship is evoked to discuss Human Resources (HR)-related issues:

... and that's useful to judge whether you encourage someone to look for a promotion or you just try and keep them motivated, or whether they're a <u>problem child</u> and you need to do something else with them.

This example demonstrates quite a condescending view of the employee, and indeed, for some, being considered a child was not helpful:

I'm actually much more motivated by being envious of someone else's success than <u>someone hitting me over the head saying 'naughty boy'</u>.

Home and family metaphors therefore serve a dual function in this data. While family-related metaphors may connote a sense of security, care, and belonging, here there is more of a sense of authoritarianism and subsequent infantilisation. In some cases, the metaphors may imply that there is a dominant parental 'voice' in the upper echelons of the Service, which is taking on a role of supervision, discipline, and schooling. The ways in which these metaphors are being used here suggest a negative evaluation of this culture, which is perceived as being infantilising. However, it is interesting to note the degree to which cynicism and potential hyperbole are used here (as in the 'naughty boy' example given above). The humorous effect that this has may somewhat mitigate the negative evaluation, or serve as a coping strategy (Plester, 2009).

Eating and food

Metaphors relating to eating and food tended to be used conventionally and were somewhat more likely to serve a positive evaluative function than a negative one.

Here are some examples of eating metaphors that were used to perform a positive evaluative function:

> ... and I don't say it flippantly when I say feedback is the <u>breakfast of champions</u>
>
> Flexibility, ability intellectually to <u>digest</u> what's going on [makes someone with real potential]
>
> If you're offering them a good, big, <u>crunchy</u> job

The first of these metaphors compares positive feedback to fortifying food, whereas the second emphasises the importance of being able to absorb or assimilate information from one's surroundings and the third describes a particular job itself in terms of a positive, yet challenging food texture, presumably implying that it's the kind of job that one can get one's teeth into.

When eating metaphors were used negatively they tended to endow the Civil Service with agency: it was often the Civil Service itself that was doing the eating, often presented as some sort of monster or machine. In the example

Table 3.4 Percentages of creative and conventional metaphors involving eating and food

Evaluation	Conventional Raw	%	Creative Raw	%	Total Raw	%
Positive evaluation	14	51.85	0	0.00	14	48.28
Negative evaluation	9	33.33	1	50.00	10	34.48
Mixed/ambiguous evaluation	2	7.41	1	50.00	3	10.34
Not clearly evaluative	2	7.41	0	0.00	2	6.90
TOTAL	27	100	2	100	29	100

below, the Civil Service itself is conceptualised as a kind of wild animal. This image imbues it with a strong degree of animacy, while simultaneously removing agency from those working within it:

> It <u>chewed them up and spat them out at the other end</u>.

This image is reiterated in the example below, which further highlights the metaphor and underscores its importance:

> Oh, well I thought they'd spit me out after about a year and a half, so the fact I've been here – that's my plan – the fact I've been here six years [...] And they will get me one day: they will <u>spit me out</u> one day, but not just at the moment.

The above example is also interesting because it seems to indicate a degree of acceptance on the part of the speaker that they will, one day, be 'spat out'. This may indicate an attitude towards work in the Civil Service that accepts its rather 'cut-throat' nature, and we will see these attitudes potentially reflected through the use of military metaphors below. It should be noted that the context also plays a role here; these are senior Civil Servants who have been successful in their careers and may not fear sudden role changes as much as a less established professional might.

Other negative uses of metaphors to do with 'eating' contained elements of infantilisation as discussed above, and some of these metaphors were also coded as referring to 'family and upbringing'. We can see examples of these below, the first of which also represents a creative, hyperbolic extension of a conventional metaphor:

> We're still on <u>liquids</u>; I'm not sure we've got to <u>solid foods</u> yet

> That should be an ideal role for somebody who's aspiring to get to be DG finance or perm sec or whatever, to really <u>cut their teeth</u>.

> How much of this do you need to <u>spoon feed</u>

Thus, metaphorical references to eating were used to evaluate the workplace culture in different ways. When they were used on their own, they generally served a positive evaluative function, but when they were used in combination with other metaphors, such as the idea of the Civil Service as a wild animal or a machine, or as a family, they presented a far more negative picture of the culture. These metaphors reflect the ambivalent views towards the Civil Service; while it can offer opportunities for development (as shown by metaphors relating to 'cutting one's teeth' or to being supported in this development through 'spoon-feeding') and rewarding ('crunchy') employment, these metaphors also connote the Service as a dangerous environment which uses people for its own ends. The metaphors shown in this section may offer interesting insights into the ways in which the valence of an evaluative metaphor may be altered by the context in which it is used, and the other metaphor types with which it is combined.

Fighting, war and physical attack, military

Metaphors falling into the category of fighting, war and physical attack and the military tended to be used conventionally, and were more likely to perform negative or mixed/ambiguous evaluation rather than positive evaluation.

The Civil Service was often conceptualised as a battleground, with employees risking physical injury from various assailants, sometimes within the Service itself:

> But I think nobody will <u>stick their head above the parapet</u> if every time they do it gets cut off. And I think you have a culture here where people have learned not to <u>stick their head above the parapet</u> because nobody's <u>covering</u> them.

Attacks could also come from outside the service:

> I mean, my permanent secretary used to say when I used to get called to select committees and the PAC, 'God, you're brilliant'. And I think, well, we spend all day every day in a council environment having the public <u>throw bricks at us</u> and the members in public. So you're more trained in that respect and you're a bit more robust.

We saw above that the Civil Service could be conceptualised negatively, as a machine or wild animal that would 'chew people up' and 'spit them out'. We see a similar view of the organisation expressed through the use of physical attack metaphors, unsurprisingly as the act of eating someone could be construed as a physical attack:

> I think the Civil Service can <u>kill</u> careers as well if people just become too comfortable and just stay on.

Table 3.5 Percentages of creative and conventional metaphors involving fighting, war and physical attack, military

Evaluation	Conventional Raw	%	Creative Raw	%	Total Raw	%
Positive evaluation	13	23.21	0	0.00	13	21.31
Negative evaluation	25	44.64	3	60.00	28	45.90
Mixed/ambiguous evaluation	18	32.14	2	40.00	20	32.79
Not clearly evaluative	0	0.00	0	0.00	0	0.00
TOTAL	56	100	5	100	61	100

The connotations of this metaphor are slightly different, as there is far more finality to being 'killed' than to being 'eaten', but ultimately 'spat out'.

Day-to-day workplace activities were often construed in terms of military metaphors, and associated weaponry:

> These are not final *wars*, they're a series of *battles*; so don't *win* too many and don't crow about them if you do, because these are ongoing relationships.

> ...*siege tactics* – I mean slow, steady, build-up preparation for a parliamentary hearing

> So using finance as an enabler rather than as a *one-dimensional hammer with which to hit people*

The last of these examples is creative in that it involves the addition of more detail into a conventional mapping. As we can see, both creative and conventional metaphors can therefore serve a similar communicative function, but as seen above, creatively used metaphors tended to perform a more striking negative evaluation.

Making progress within the Service could be conceptualised as earning promotions in the armed forces:

> You have to just *earn your stripes*; you just have to earn your credibility.

But this could also lead to in-fighting between members of the service, with colleagues 'fighting each other for turf', as one participant commented. Another participant drew metaphorical parallels between the army and working in the Civil Service, resulting in a creative extended scenario.

> But generally you're trained. It's mission analysis. What's my commander's intent? What are the tasks implicit in that? What are the constraints? And question four, the most important question: has the tactical situation changed? And as long as you understand your commander's intent and the constraints on your action are what they are, you do what you think is most likely to achieve that outcome.

In some cases, military metaphors were used to express the view that one often needed to keep a low profile:

> I think you have a culture here where people have learned not to *stick their head above the parapet* because nobody's *covering* them.

> No, I found out a long time ago in my little life that doing very unsexy, boring but important things, if you're a girl, it stops you getting *shot* quite as much as if you go after the really big, glamorous stuff that the boys think they should do. So that's how I've *survived*.

Military metaphors have been shown to be prevalent in people's discussions of their careers more generally, where they encapsulate notions of hierarchy, fighting and resistance (El-Sawad, 2005).

What is interesting about these metaphors is the extent to which they seem playful, humorous or hyperbolic, and there are hardly any references to people getting hurt. Like the family metaphors above, this has the effect of mitigating what would otherwise seem a very violent and bloody scene. It should be noted that, just as we saw with the 'eating' examples above, the context also plays a role here; these are senior Civil Servants who have been successful in their careers. They may see such 'warfare' as having less of an effect on them than on more junior colleagues, in much the same way as a military general may not need to go to the front lines. It would be interesting to explore the extent to which similar metaphorical language is used by workers of different levels.

Sport and ludic pastimes

Metaphors referring to sport and ludic pastimes were more conventional and tended to be used to perform negative and mixed/ambiguous evaluation, with some being used for positive evaluation.

As with the war metaphors mentioned above, the majority of the sport and ludic pastimes metaphors were used to perform both positive and negative evaluation. One might expect war metaphors to be more negative and sport and ludic pastimes metaphors to be more positive but in our data, they were more mixed/ambiguous. Some were used to frame the Civil Service in a positive way as in this example where the speaker is conceptualising themselves as a fencer:

> But it is a *cut and thrust*, and I do like the *sparring* of it. I love the intellectual *sparring* that is negotiation.

Table 3.6 Percentages of creative and conventional metaphors involving sport and ludic pastimes

Evaluation	Conventional Raw	%	Creative Raw	%	Total Raw	%
Positive evaluation	6	16.22	3	37.50	9	20.00
Negative evaluation	13	35.14	3	37.50	16	35.56
Mixed/ambiguous evaluation	14	37.84	2	25.00	16	35.56
Not clearly evaluative	4	10.81	0	0.00	4	8.89
TOTAL	37	100	8	100	45	100

46 Creative metaphors and evaluation

Here, the fighting is merely 'sparring', which does not carry violent connotations. The speaker also makes their enjoyment of the process explicit.

Some speakers used metaphors from this category in a way that was reminiscent of those in the 'family, upbringing, and the home' category in terms of how they conveyed ideas of coaching and support. In the example below, we see a creatively extended metaphor which draws on the fairly conventional idea that managing subordinates is similar to the role of a sports coach. Here, the scene is made specific to tennis, which is slightly unconventional, and the speaker extends this further by referring to a specific feature tennis coaching, i.e. that the coach sometimes needs to let the pupil win in order for them to learn:

> *I've had to change my language more, and rather than saying 'there's a better way', it's almost encouraging, supportive. It's a bit like a <u>tennis coach</u> or anything else like that. <u>A tennis coach is going to beat their pupil every time</u>: if they do that, they're not going to teach them anything. The trick is to come down a bit to allow the other person to step up*

However, these lacked the potentially infantilising connotations that we saw in the 'family' metaphors, and convey more of a supportive, facilitative role.

Metaphors from this category were also used to describe the everyday activities within the Service, with highly conventional metaphors such as '<u>high hurdle</u>', '<u>drop the ball</u>', and '<u>tackling</u>' problems being frequently employed. Life in the Civil Service was frequently conceptualised as a game, with project '<u>kick-offs</u>', colleagues who may or may not be '<u>team players</u>', and the need to '<u>play the game</u>'. This has interesting implications when compared to the positively valenced military metaphors described above, as it may indicate that a sense of competition (whether expressed through sport or through war metaphors) is seen as positive. However, some examples in this category were rather more creative, often drawing on more sedentary pastimes. These more unconventional examples are often more complex, drawing on extended scenarios to explain situations in a vivid, marked fashion:

> *What's the <u>picture</u> of what I'm trying to get to, and how do I navigate people to that <u>picture</u>? And transformational journeys are always about a holistic view of the world. It's not just about a new finance process; it's well, what does that mean for people, processes, policies, organisations, technology? How do you make that holistic thing tie together? How do you explain to people what this <u>jigsaw box lid</u> looks like that this is <u>one piece</u> of, and then keep taking people back to the <u>jigsaw box lid</u>?*

This example (which we also saw in Chapter 2) is particularly interesting given that the creatively used metaphor involving a jigsaw puzzle box lid links back to the highly conventional metaphor of a 'picture' at the beginning of the explanation. While the metaphor of a 'picture' is not particularly creative in isolation, its proximity to the more vivid, creatively used metaphor of the jigsaw box lid appears to make its metaphoricity more salient. The idea that the metaphoricity of a given word is not fixed and can be affected by both the context and the co-text has been discussed at length in the metaphor literature (see, for example, Cameron & Low, 2004; Müller, 2009).

This next example also conceptualises work in the Civil Service as play, but the image here is different again to the more conventional, active examples described above:

What typically happens is that people will go from here to another department, or they might go to an arm's length body where you can get a balance, you get more autonomy possibly, you might get paid more, <u>you might have a smaller train set but you get to use the controls.</u>

Here, there is no sense of competition, but neither is there the idea of collaboration implied in the jigsaw box example. There, management was described in terms of leading people to see a particular picture. Here, however, the 'game' is more solitary, with unilateral control in the hands of the speaker.

Also, these last two examples provide insights into the nature of the Civil Service workplace. In both cases, there appears to be a 'correct' way of doing things; either there is a pre-defined picture that can only be produced in one specific way, or there is the implication of a defined journey on rails with no opportunity to deviate from this path. In this image, effective management within the Service is conceptualised as placing the train on these rails and moving it in the right direction. We see further examples of this in the 'Journey' category below. Finally, we can draw parallels between some of the metaphors in this section, and those of the 'Family, upbringing, and the home' metaphors discussed above. A picture is beginning to emerge of a workplace described with references to childhood, growing up, and play; while these metaphors may seem jarring presented alongside the more militaristic or violent metaphors described above, these, too, do not connote a real sense of 'danger'; even when people are being 'spat out', as discussed, they seem rather equanimous about it. Perhaps there is a tendency for these metaphors to be used as a means of coming to terms with the pressures of the job; if such tasks can be described as a game, possibly played in a family context, they may become somewhat less onerous.

Health and injury

Health and injury metaphors tended to be used in conventional ways to perform negative evaluation.

Health and injury metaphors tended to refer more to illness than to physical injuries, which may support the idea that while there are 'violent' scenes used to refer to the Civil Service work culture, these rarely lead to real damage

48 *Creative metaphors and evaluation*

Table 3.7 Percentages of creative and conventional metaphors involving health and injury

Evaluation	Conventional Raw	%	Creative Raw	%	Total Raw	%
Positive evaluation	1	7.14	0	0.00	1	6.67
Negative evaluation	10	71.43	1	100.00	11	73.33
Mixed/ambiguous evaluation	3	21.43	0	0.00	3	20.00
Not clearly evaluative	0	0.00	0	0.00	0	0.00
TOTAL	14	100	1	100	15	100

– or at least, if they do, it is not desirable that this should be made explicit. This observation was borne out in our discussion of the metaphors related to fighting, war, and physical attack above, where it was noted that explicit references to injury or death are not made. As we saw above, metaphorical references to war and fighting tended to be presented in a positive way and their negative aspects were downplayed. In contrast, the metaphors in the health and injury category were almost entirely negative or mixed/ambiguous.

Health and injury-related metaphors were sometimes used to describe individuals, and these were usually very conventional. Speakers described having '*jaundiced*' views or being '*scarred* for life'. Equally conventionally, broader concepts could be referred to as 'unhealthy' (there were no references to things being 'healthy', conversely):

> It's <u>unhealthy</u> for the totality of the organisation if you've got too many people coming into it now

> That's just creating a very <u>unhealthy</u> tension

The first example is particularly interesting as it conceptualises the Civil Service itself as something that can be healthy or unhealthy. Again, the Service is given animacy, but whereas previous examples of this did so in a negative way (conceptualising the organisation as something that could 'chew people up'), here it is framed as a being that requires healthcare. This view can be developed to allow for conceptualisations of managers as doctors:

> What [they] did [...] was buy a lot of people and <u>inject</u> them in the system

This view is extended to the highly innovative and creative image of organ transplant surgery being used to describe moving into the Civil Service from another field, which is also notable for the depersonalising effects of the person being 'transplanted':

So I think there is a feeling that private sector good, public sector incompetent; and if people turn up expecting to be able to rule the world, that's just not going to happen. And the public sector is for things that are different to what the private sector is for, and you have to really [...] understand the nature of the beast that you're in in order to make a difference. And if you can't do that then you won't make it. Someone described it to me [...] as <u>organ rejection</u>, which is quite graphic but I can see what they mean. So fortunately I wasn't rejected.

Similarly, medical procedures were used to conceptualise solving problems within the Civil Service. Here, again, the Service is viewed as having a 'body' that can be ill or injured, while its senior members take the role of doctors who can provide medical care:

Having done that very detailed review in the first year, we had a far smoother passage last year because <u>we'd excised an awful lot of poison</u>, I suppose – an awful lot of bad things.

Machinery, industry, and manual labour

Metaphors relating to machinery, industry, and manual labour were used relatively more positively, again with the majority being used conventionally.

From senior Service members being considered doctors and surgeons, we now turn to another category which provided insights into how speakers saw their roles. Here, the Civil Service was conceptualised as a machine, and working within it was described in terms of manual labour. As with the previous categories, many of the metaphors used here were highly conventional. Different sectors are described as having '*tools*' that can be brought to bear on Civil Service work, relationships can be '*built*', and problems need to be '*fixed*'. However, these conventional metaphors were often used in creative ways.

Table 3.8 Percentages of creative and conventional metaphors involving machinery, industry, and manual labour

Evaluation	Conventional Raw	%	Creative Raw	%	Total Raw	%
Positive evaluation	30	47.62	1	14.29	31	44.29
Negative evaluation	21	33.33	2	28.57	23	32.86
Mixed evaluation	5	7.94	4	57.14	9	12.86
Not clearly evaluative	7	11.11	0	0.00	7	10.00
TOTAL	63	100	7	100	70	100

For example, here the speaker playfully reappropriates and extends the conventional idiom of 'reinventing the wheel':

> So if somebody's <u>invented the wheel, just go and get the wheel</u>: you don't need to do it yourself.

Here, too, we see the conventional idea of 'going with/against the grain' being reformulated in more unusual ways:

> One thing I've learnt [...] is, if you want to effect change in an organisation, spend time understanding the culture of the organisation first, because unless you've got an absolutely massively powerful mandate to <u>cut across the grain</u> to effect change – and some organisations want that sort of change – in the public sector you've got to <u>go with the grain</u> and <u>make the grain work with the change</u>.

Similarly, while the idea of 'filling in a gap' is a conventional way of expressing fixing a problem, this speaker reformulates this conventional metaphor in a creative way:

> You've got a <u>hole</u> – how do you make sure you <u>fill the hole in</u> without anybody really noticing you had a <u>hole</u> in the first place?

This speaker also draws on a conventional metaphor, but draws attention to it, encouraging the listener to consider the metaphorical implications of what has been said:

> And also doing submissions: a lot of them didn't know how you <u>craft</u> submissions to ministers. <u>And I use the word 'craft' specifically</u>.

These metaphors were also used to conceptualise the Civil Service itself, when it was considered to be an industry:

> ... in the <u>engine room</u> when I was training

This gave rise to various industrial processes being used to describe professional activities

> We need to <u>harness</u> their energy, enthusiasm, and hopefully <u>temper</u> it with wisdom;

However, sometimes interviewees depersonalised themselves and/or their colleagues by conceptualising them as being *part* of a machine, as opposed to working within an industrial context:

> You've got to be a very, very strong <u>self-contained little unit</u> to make sure it all <u>works</u> all the time.

Creative metaphors and evaluation 51

Thus, the metaphors in this category could be used to express the varying degrees of agency experienced by the participants in their workplace environment. This was extended to prospective workers within the Service, who were described as being '*sifted*' for interview.

A particular metaphor which was used by some participants was that of a 'lever'. Here, participants were conceptualising themselves as having control over the 'machine' of the Civil Service, as opposed to being a part of it themselves.

> *So most of what you do is about influence and persuasion. There are very few hard <u>levers</u>.*

> *I've set up a mentoring or buddy system for myself with some trusted people I can go to and talk to about where I'm not <u>pressing the right levers</u> or things aren't having the right sort of impact.*

These examples represent different attitudes towards the flexibility of the Civil Service, with the second example implying that there are objectively 'correct' procedures to follow in opposition to the first.

We have seen in this section that metaphors relating to manual labour and industry were used, often in quite creative ways, to present the Civil Service as a machine or industrial process that needs to be maintained and operated in an appropriate way in order to maximise its efficiency. Colleagues are evaluated positively when they operate the machine well or form efficient parts of the machine. Of particular interest here, however, is the relative levels of agency given to Civil Service employees. We saw above how workers within the Civil Service could be conceptualised as 'outputs' of a process or 'organs' to be transplanted for the good of the organisation, but the metaphors discussed here tend to give the speaker a degree of agency in the process. This may be due to the interviewees' seniority, and future research could usefully compare metaphor use across different levels of the Service.

Types of movement that do not refer to journeys; constraints to movement

As we saw above, movement metaphors that did not refer to journeys were the most frequent category in the dataset. Metaphors relating to movement were generally conventional and used to perform both positive and negative evaluation. However, when these metaphors were used creatively, they were more likely to perform negative or mixed/ambiguous evaluation.

A good example of a creatively used metaphor being used to perform ambiguous or mixed/ambiguous evaluation is as follows:

> *So I suppose, as people rotate round, some will <u>spin off the merry-go-round</u> and <u>shoot off</u> back to the private sector.*

52   *Creative metaphors and evaluation*

Table 3.9 Percentages of creative and conventional metaphors involving other types of movement that do not refer to journeys; constraints to movement

Evaluation	Conventional Raw	%	Creative Raw	%	Total Raw	%
Positive evaluation	64	31.53	1	4.00	65	28.51
Negative evaluation	73	35.96	10	40.00	83	36.40
Mixed/ambiguous evaluation	36	17.73	13	52.00	49	21.49
Not clearly evaluative	30	14.78	1	4.00	31	13.60
TOTAL	203	100	25	100	228	100

This metaphor implies that the people being discussed have no control. The use of the merry-go-round also implies that while there is a great deal of movement they are not actually going anywhere, and at one point and they may inadvertently 'shoot off' or choose to do so. There is an interesting contrast in this metaphor between the 'fun', childhood experience of the merry-go-round and the stressful nature of the work environment. The metaphor implies the futility of the endeavour mixed with a sense that it should not be taken seriously and that it is just a form of entertainment. This may relate to the playful, family-related metaphors discussed above.

As with some of the metaphors referred to in the manual labour and industry section, this metaphor expresses an ambiguous attitude towards agency. Whilst some people may be thrown from the merry-go-round, others may choose to jump off. Other examples of metaphors being used to refer to agency whilst conveying mixed/ambiguous evaluation include the following, which contrasts the moving of oneself with the idea of being 'moved by others':

> So I believe you should <u>step away</u> before someone asks you to go.

In other cases participants made use of differing degrees of agency within the same utterance:

> I think there's lots of examples of people who have <u>parachuted into</u> the wrong place – let's just say department x – they're a bright young finance person <u>parachuted in</u>. It's easy to get lost. You need some kind of support structure around you. So they'd be the caveats.

In this example, there is a change between the two references to parachuting. In the first, the people are doing the parachuting themselves, thus implying a certain degree of agency (although it could be argued that in the act of parachuting itself there is a limited degree of agency because once they have jumped out of the aeroplane, the parachutist is very much at the mercy of the prevailing winds). In the second however, they are 'being' parachuted. The implication here is that they have not had any choice over where they are going or over whether they wanted to jump out of the plane in the first place. This example is also reminiscent of the military examples above.

Some participants used movement metaphors to talk about their own agency in their career paths. Sometimes this referred only to the level of agency in their own experience:

> *I wasn't running away; I was running towards something.*

Or their frustration at a lack of agency:

> *All the people who've come in from outside who go 'what on earth?' But most of us have hit the wall at nine months, and that's the point where you either decide to jump or you get it. And it's quite tough until then.*

> *And it's because you just end up being sucked into this world where you may have months at a time of being at your desk at seven in the morning and not leaving until midnight*

And at other times, participants used movement metaphors to talk about the agency that they exert over other people and situations:

> *I used to see myself as a leader, in many respects, because you can lead your colleagues, can't you? And you can corral and push ideas, etc. so that everybody gets behind it.*

As well as movement in general, some of the metaphors focused on the *manner* of movement involved. These references to manner of movement were often used to convey negative evaluation:

> *And you see people, especially from the private sector, come into government, they jump every eighteen months or two years, and the reason they do that is because they don't want to deliver anything;*

> *Ministers love people from the private sector to come in and say, 'You're a bunch of idiots. The Civil Service is useless. I could show them how to do it in twelve months flat. Pay me £200,000 and I'll do it.' And they all come into the Cabinet Office and they all wander, strut around, make lots of speeches, set lots of challenging questions; but they never hang around because they know they can't, because they know they're never going to change it that way. The only way to change anything in the Civil Service is from the grassroots up, basically.*

54 *Creative metaphors and evaluation*

> *I guess it's mildly frustrating. I think one of the things that helps is that I tend not to get stressed or frustrated, so you just have to accept that that's the system and try and work it as quickly as possible. And part of that, actually, is knowing the people to talk to and how to work it effectively. So I think if you try and <u>gate-crash</u> it, as I think the former CFO who recruited me tried to, there's a high risk of failure, I think.*

These participants clearly disapprove of colleagues who 'jump', 'strut around' and 'gate crash'. These are very vivid images and provide insights into a workplace culture where it may not necessarily be deemed appropriate to be overly combative. This would be in line with the use of family-based metaphors seen above, which are not compatible with ideas of 'jumping' and 'gate-crashing'.

Journeys and/or movement from one place to another

A more specific application of the movement metaphors is through the idea of a journey. These metaphors tended to be used in conventional ways, where just over half were used positively. However, the few instances where they were used creatively appeared to follow a slightly different pattern in that they were used to perform slightly more negative or mixed evaluation.

These metaphors ranged from explicit references to journeys and travelling...

> *I've been on a bit of a transformational <u>journey</u> [...] and transformational journeys are always about a holistic view of the world*

> *think strategically about <u>direction of travel</u>*

> *I was quite resistant to going into policy at the start because I thought that was going off my <u>career path</u>*

> *We must let people have a clear vision of <u>where we're going</u>*

Table 3.10 Percentages of creative and conventional metaphors involving journeys and/or movement from one place to another

Evaluation	Conventional Raw	%	Creative Raw	%	Total Raw	%
Positive evaluation	12	52.17	3	37.50	15	48.39
Negative evaluation	5	21.74	2	25.00	7	22.58
Mixed evaluation	5	21.74	3	37.50	8	25.81
Not clearly evaluative	1	4.35	0	0.00	1	3.23
TOTAL	23	100	8	100	31	100

> *I think it is showing that there is a <u>path</u> and the Civil Service will invest in your getting that experience*

…to references to the processes and activities associated with them, for example luggage, embarking and disembarking etc:

> *So the <u>on-boarding</u> process, or how we acclimatise people to our culture*
>
> *… <u>navigate</u> the complexity of the rules*
>
> *I had five years' worth of <u>baggage</u> I needed to <u>unload</u>*

Interestingly, it is not only people who go on journeys, but the departments in which they are working, and even the Civil Service as a whole.

> *Finance has shifted a lot since this millennium really, but it's still on a <u>journey</u> that's got further to go.*
>
> *To be fair to the Civil Service, it is on a <u>journey</u> to improve its execution capability*

The journeys here are generally being conceptualised in a positive way; the pathways are clearly defined and progress is generally smooth. In contrast, the only clearly negative use of the journey metaphor was one in which the journey was by no means planned or direct, and this was conveyed through the creative inclusion of a manner of movement verb:

> *So [NAME], when I was there, it would just be a <u>ramble</u> through [the Minister's] head […] even though you'd have an agenda*

The metaphor here is being used to convey negative evaluation of the chairing skills of the individual involved.

What becomes clear in this section is that being on a pre-determined path and following established directions tends to be evaluated positively within the Civil Service, and that Civil Servants benefit from being directed along this path. This coheres with the family, upbringing, and the home metaphors mentioned above, in that they entail a degree of prescribed behaviours and 'linear' progression. It also relates to the negative evaluation of those who 'jump around' exemplified in the 'Movement' section above, as these people are deviating from their established path.

Nature and the natural world

Metaphors referring to nature and the natural world as a whole did not demonstrate a clear tendency towards either positive or negative evaluation.

56 *Creative metaphors and evaluation*

However, we did find that conventional nature-related metaphors were more likely to perform positive evaluation while creative nature-related metaphors were more likely to perform negative or mixed evaluation.

Many of the positive metaphors in this category related to ideas of 'growing people' as if they were plants, with several references to the ideas of 'growing your own', which suggests that the speakers attached value to developing personnel on their own terms, within their departments. Plant-related metaphors were also apparent in descriptions of people 'flourishing' or 'blossoming'. Other conventional uses of metaphor appeared to liken the working environment of the Civil Service to the natural environment. We can see this in the following examples:

> *I think fertile ground might be Cabinet Office*
>
> *But they've sort of got this symbiotic relationship with Civil Servants*
>
> *I've tended to have a history also of jobs growing around me*

Within this category, we also found a number of metaphorical scenarios, which appeared to perform negative or mixed evaluation. Here is an example of one such scenario in which a speaker refers to the capricious nature of one of their managers:

> *And he's the sort of manager who'll say 'bring me a pebble', and you go and find him a pebble. And he'll say, 'no, no, no, bigger', 'no, no, no, rounder', 'no, no, no, different'. And three weeks later he'll actually decide what he wanted was a half brick. He's a bit like that.*

Here the speaker uses an imaginary scenario to convey the idea that it is virtually impossible to please their manager as he always wants something more or different than what they have done for him.

In this next example, the speaker offers a mixed evaluation of their own performance when running a department:

Table 3.11 Percentages of creative and conventional metaphors involving nature and the natural world

Evaluation	Conventional Raw	%	Creative Raw	%	Total Raw	%
Positive evaluation	18	41.86	0	0.00	18	33.33
Negative evaluation	12	27.91	7	63.64	19	35.19
Mixed evaluation	6	13.95	3	27.27	9	16.67
Not clearly evaluative	7	16.28	1	9.09	8	14.81
TOTAL	43	100	11	100	54	100

Creative metaphors and evaluation 57

> *I inherited a complete dog* and *left it a slightly better dog* by the time I left. *It probably wasn't a dog when I left it*

The expression 'I inherited a complete dog of an xxxx' is generally used to refer to the fact that the person working on the project before them made a mess of it and that it subsequently needed to be fixed. This speaker goes on to say that they 'left it a slightly better dog', indicating that they had improved it to some extent; they then go on to say that 'it probably wasn't a dog when I left it', presumably to imply that they had fixed the problem by the time they left the post. The 'complete' dog expression is not usually extended in this way but the scenario that is created through its extension provides a memorable account of the disaster that they inherited and their success in resolving the issue.

Within this category, a number of uses of metaphor to convey negative or mixed evaluation involved extended metaphorical scenarios. Indeed, the extension of the 'elephant in the room' idiom, as we saw in Chapter 2, was used to critique the fact that members of the Civil Service were (or at least pretended to be) oblivious to major problems that were staring them in the face. These scenarios allow for a rich description of the event or behaviour that is being evaluated, which perhaps explains why they were well suited to conveying complex, mixed forms of evaluation.

Actions and experiences not included in other categories

In this final section, we consider the more general category of 'general actions and experiences'. This category included metaphors that referred in some way to an action or experience that did not fit neatly into any of the categories above. As we can see in Table 3.12, both the creative and conventional examples of these metaphors tended to be used negatively.

Examples of negative uses of metaphor in this category include the following:

> They make *a hell of a hash of it*
>
> *I completely lost my sense of self and was totally drained of confidence in that role.*

When these metaphors were used positively, they were relatively more likely to be conventional, as we can see in the following example:

> *You just sort of absorb management skills as you get into managerial positions*

The example below demonstrates the creative use of metaphor for negative evaluation. As discussed in Chapter 2, the participant is creatively drawing on the conventional idea of 'rearranging the deckchairs on the Titanic' and

Table 3.12 Percentages of creative and conventional metaphors involving actions and experiences not included in other categories

Evaluation	Conventional Raw	%	Creative Raw	%	Total Raw	%
Positive evaluation	21	21.88	5	22.73	26	22.03
Negative evaluation	44	45.83	11	50.00	55	46.61
Mixed evaluation	19	19.79	5	22.73	24	20.34
Not clearly evaluative	12	12.50	1	4.55	13	11.02
TOTAL	96	100	22	100	118	100

combining this with the idea of throwing objects in the air to cause chaos to negatively evaluate a colleague.

> She did the traditional sort of *chuck it all up in the air*, so get all the deckchairs and throw them up in the air, cause chaos for a year and a half and then leave, and that's basically what she did.

Creatively used metaphors in this category were also used to convey mixed/ ambiguous evaluation. For example, one participant described the relationship that existed between the Civil Service and the politicians with reference to 'stroking'. While it is conventional to talk about egos being stroked, the metonymic underspecification makes it more striking and memorable:

> But they've sort of got this symbiotic relationship with Civil Servants where, although they say they want delivery skills, they don't just want a sort of political environment; they kind of like <u>being stroked</u> and they've got people that are quite good at <u>stroking</u> them.

Conclusion

In this chapter, we have seen that in conversations about the workplace, the use of metaphor was in most cases associated with some form of evaluation, that this was particularly true of creatively used metaphors and that creatively used metaphors were proportionately more likely to perform negative evaluation than conventional metaphors. The extent to which negative evaluation was associated with the use of creatively used metaphor varied across the different metaphor categories.

Note

1 The order in which the metaphor categories are presented in this table corresponds to the order in which they are discussed below. This order was chosen as it allows

us to draw attention to noteworthy relationships that we observed between some of the categories.

References

Cameron, L., & Low, G. (2004). Figurative variation in episodes of educational talk and text. *European Journal of English Studies*, *8*(3), 355–373.

El-Sawad, A. (2005). Becoming a lifer? Unlocking career through metaphor. *Journal of Occupational and Organizational Psychology*, *78*(1), 23–41.

Gibbs Jr, R. W. (2005). *Embodiment and cognitive science*. Cambridge University Press.

Müller, C. (2009). *Metaphors dead and alive, sleeping and waking, a dynamic view*. University of Chicago Press.

Okonski, L., Gibbs, R. W., & Chen, E. (2020). *Metaphor in multimodal creativity*. In: Performing Metaphorical Creativity across Modes and Contexts / [ed] Laura Hidalgo-Downing, Blanca Kraljevic Mujic, Amsterdam/Philadephia: John Benjamins Publishing Company, 2020, p. 19–41.

Plester, B. (2009). Healthy humour: Using humour to cope at work. *Kōtuitui: New Zealand Journal of Social Sciences Online*, *4*(1), 89–102. https://doi.org/10.1080/1177083X.2009.9522446

4 Conclusion: 'As people rotate round, some will spin off the merry-go-round and shoot off back to the private sector'

In this study, we have explored the role played by creative and conventional uses of metaphor in expressing positive and negative evaluation about a particular workplace: the British Civil Service. We have seen that the metaphors used tended to serve a predominantly evaluative function. Creatively used metaphors were proportionately more likely than conventional metaphors to perform an evaluative function, particularly when the evaluation was negative or mixed/ambiguous. The analysis of these metaphors provides insights into the (sometimes critical) views that Civil Servants hold about their workplace experiences. This finding builds on earlier work (Fuoli et al., 2021) where we found an association between metaphor and negative evaluation and between creatively used metaphor and evaluation in general. In that study we did not find a relationship between *creatively used* metaphor and *negative* evaluation, but this relationship was observed in the current study. As we suggested in the introduction, this finding may be due to the fact that in this study we are focusing on personal emotionally-charged experiences. Another additional finding that we have made is that mixed/ambiguous evaluation is also more likely to be associated with the creative use of metaphor than positive evaluation. This may reflect the fact metaphors allow for plurality of interpretations, and with creatively used metaphors there is less common ground between the speaker and the listener which allows for a wider set of potential interpretations which is less constrained by convention.

It should be noted that the way in which speakers used metaphor is likely to have been influenced by the context in which the metaphors were produced, i.e. the research interview. They were being asked to evaluate their workplace in a confidential, informal one-to-one conversation. Many personal reactions and strong feelings are being expressed through these conversations, and we can assume that the interviewees were able to be candid because they felt reasonably comfortable with the interviewer. It is unlikely that they would have expressed their feelings in this way in a more formal setting.

Despite these caveats, metaphor analysis provides intriguing insights into the ways in which senior Civil Servants conceptualise their work. Throughout our analysis, there has been a sense of ambivalence, with metaphors that may traditionally be considered quite negative being used to describe positive experiences, and vice versa. Our work gives a different insight into working in the Civil Service and thus may aid recruitment into the Civil Service from other sectors (Urban & Thomas, 2022), and will give people from other public and private sectors an appreciation of working in the Civil Service.

These findings also have interesting implications for metaphor theory. Our findings provide more nuance to the link between evaluation, creativity and metaphor already identified in our previous work. As we have shown through the examples given, creativity often comes through subverting the norms of use of a particular metaphor category, or altering the valence from its conventional use (e.g. military metaphors being positive, or family metaphors being negative).

Our study has some limitations. The number of participants in the study was relatively small, so care must be taken not to generalise too much from these interviews. On the other hand, this relatively small dataset allowed for a detailed and in-depth qualitative analysis of the metaphors produced, and of the ways in which they were used to perform positive and negative evaluation. Another drawback of our study is that it was focused solely on one workplace culture (that of the UK Civil Service), and it is therefore difficult to ascertain the extent to which these metaphorical framings are unique to that particular workplace culture, or whether they are typical of workplace cultures more generally. More research could usefully be conducted into other workplace settings in other countries, in order to establish the extent to which our findings are reflective of this particular workplace. Finally, our study has focused exclusively on metaphor, and there are likely to have been other linguistic mechanisms (e.g. tense, aspect, modality) that the participants employed to describe and evaluate their experiences. A more rounded linguistic analysis might shed further light on the experiences of these individuals.

Despite its limitations, our study has provided insight into the rich and varied experiences of this group of people in their workplace. It has shown the myriad ways in which people push at the boundaries of linguistic creativity in their efforts to describe the qualitative nature of their experiences. It has also shown that metaphor can be a powerful tool for the nuanced expression of complex and ambiguous evaluation, particularly when it is used creatively.

References

Fuoli, M., Littlemore, J., & Turner, S. (2021). Sunken Ships and Screaming Banshees: Metaphor and evaluation in film reviews. *English Language and Linguistics, 26*(1), 75–103.

Urban, J., & Thomas, A. (2022). Opening Up: How to strengthen the civil service through external recruitment. Institute for Government, 1.

Index

abstract concepts 2–3, 9
agency 41–42, 51–54
animacy 42, 48
appraisal 4
appraisal 4
appropriateness 8, 20

basic meaning 15
basic metaphorical mapping 23
basic sense 15, 25
behaviour 3–4, 9, 21, 31, 55

civil service culture 26
coding 16–17
compactness hypothesis 4
conceptual metaphor 19–23, 28
conduit metaphor 20–23
connotation 44–46
contextual meaning 15
contrast 30–33
conventional mapping 9, 33, 44
conventional metaphorical expression 20
conventional metaphorical idea 18, 25
conventional metaphorical mapping 19–20
conventionalised metaphorical correspondence 3
conventionalised metaphorical relationship 3
corpus 2–4, 10, 17
creative extended scenario 44
creative extension process 23
creative metaphor production 4
creative metaphor type 14

creative metaphor use 17–18
creative metaphorical scenario 33
creative use of metaphor 21, 25–26, 33, 58–60
creative use of metaphor vs creative metaphor 33

dehumanisation 51
depersonalisation 26
discourse community 3

elicitation 7
emotional closeness 3
emotional experience 1–6
evaluation 35–61
evaluation in film reviews 4–5, 9, 17, 24, 37
evaluation involving extended metaphorical scenarios 44–46, 57
evaluative function of metaphor 4–7, 32, 39–42, 60
existing mappings 19–20
exploitation of one-off source domains 8–9
extended analogies 31–34
extended metaphor 20, 31–33, 37, 44–46, 57
extension of conventional metaphor 3, 19–20–23, 31–33, 37, 44–51, 56

figurative language in emotional communication 2
functions performed by metaphor 2, 39

genre 17, 31,33, 37

human behaviour 8
hyperbole 21, 24, 33, 41

identification procedure for creative uses of metaphor 17–32
identification procedure for evaluation 32–33
identification procedure for metaphor 14–17
idiom 2, 20, 21–22, 24, 27,31
idiomatic expression 21, 27, 31
implicit culture 10
inexpressibility hypothesis 4
infantilisation 41–42
interview procedure 14

language play 17
levels of abstraction 20
linguistic creativity 61
linguistic metaphor 15
literal language 4

manner of movement 53, 55
metaphor analysis 60
metaphor category 16, 37–38
metaphor elicitation 7
metaphor identification 14–17
metaphor identification procedure 14–17
metaphor in educational discourse 5
metaphor in everyday language use 6
metaphor in film reviews 17
metaphorical creativity 22
metaphorical evaluation 5
metaphorical framing 61
metaphorical idiom 2, 20, 21–22, 24, 27,31
metaphorical mapping 18–23, 33
metaphorical mode of engagement 3
metaphorical movement 17
metaphorical scenario 31–32, 57
metaphorical scene 3
metaphorical space 28
metaphoricity 16, 47
metaphors referring to journeys 55–57

metaphors relating to eating and drinking 41–43
metaphors relating to family, upbringing and the home 39–41
metaphors relating to fighting, war, physical attack and the military 43–45
metaphors relating to health and injury 47–49
metaphors relating to machinery, industry and manual labour 49–51
metaphors relating to sport and ludic pastimes 45–47
metaphors relating to types of movement and constraints to movement 51–53
metonymic exemplar 30
metonymic relationship 27
metonymic underspecification 58
metonymy 27–28, 33
mixed evaluation 33, 37–38, 54, 56–58
mood state 6

narrative 32
negative emotion 5–6, 32, 37
non-metaphorical idiom 2
novel mapping 18
novel metaphor 9
novelty 8, 18

one-off source domain 8, 9
organisational culture 6

part-whole metonymic relationship 27
personification 29, 33
physical experience 2, 4, 37
polarity of an emotional experience 5
positive emotion 5, 6
positive evaluation 5, 32, 36–45
positive mood state 6
primary metaphor 20

recontextualisation 24, 33

sensory language 2, 5
sharing of emotional experiences 2
source domain 8–9

taxonomy of creative metaphor types 17–33
twice-true metaphor 29

underspecification 58

vividness hypothesis 4

workplace culture 4, 6, 9, 39–40, 54, 61
workplace environment 4, 36, 51
workplace experience 1, 6–7, 9–10, 60